CELESTE HOLM SYNDROME

CELESTE HOLM

SYNDROME

ON CHARACTER ACTORS FROM HOLLYWOOD'S GOLDEN AGE

DAVID LAZAR

UNIVERSITY OF NEBRASKA PRESS   LINCOLN

Acknowledgments for the use of
previously published material appear
on page ix, which constitutes an
extension of the copyright page.

Library of Congress
Cataloging-in-Publication Data
Names: Lazar, David, 1957– author.
Title: Celeste Holm syndrome: on
character actors from Hollywood's
golden age / David Lazar.
Description: Lincoln: University
of Nebraska Press, [2020]
Identifiers: LCCN 2020008833
ISBN 9781496200457 (paperback)
ISBN 9781496224385 (epub)
ISBN 9781496224392 (mobi)
ISBN 9781496224408 (pdf)
Subjects: LCSH: Motion picture
actors and actresses—United
States—Biography. | Characters and
characteristics in motion pictures.
Classification: LCC PN2285 .L39 2020 |
DDC 791.4302/80922 [B]—dc23
LC record available at
https://lccn.loc.gov/2020008833

Set in Adobe Text by
Mikala R. Kolander.
Designed by N. Putens.

What does the truth look like?
It's between appearing and disappearing.

—From *Detective*, Godard

A man is a method, a progressive
arrangement, a selecting principle.

—Emerson

CONTENTS

ACKNOWLEDGMENTS

Thank you to the editors of the following periodicals in which my essays first appeared:

Cincinnati Review: "My Two Oscars: On Wit and Melancholy"
Fourth Genre: "Martin Balsam: The Best Possible Arnold Burns"
Superstition Review: "Celeste Holm Syndrome: The Eyes of Sister Scholastica"

An earlier version of "My Family Romance" appeared in my book *The Body of Brooklyn* (University of Iowa Press, 2003) as "My Little Heroes"—it has been substantially revised.

I am grateful to the John Simon Guggenheim Foundation for the fellowship that helped me in the early stages of this manuscript.

And thank you to the following friends, family, and associates who aided me, directly or indirectly, with this book: Alyce Miller, William Fraser, Patsy Kelly, Martin McGovern, Alicia Christenson, Lois Zamora, Scott Lazar, Cathleen Calbert,

Mary Cappello, Mike Mazurki; and to my parents, Leo and Rhoda Lazar, who in my forlorn memories are watching some melodrama from the '40s in their small bedroom in Brooklyn.

This book is dedicated to Scott Lazar, who accompanied me in our teens on our epic trips to the Bleeker Street Theater, the Thalia, the New Yorker, the Art, the Cinema Village, the Carnegie Hall Cinema . . .

INTRODUCTION

When I started writing about character actors, everyone I know who knows movies and actors asked me if I was writing about Thelma Ritter. There's royalty to that, a kind of character actor superstardom. It also made me not want to write about Thelma Ritter, since I've been resisting the grains of pressure and expectation since I was young enough to know who Thelma Ritter was, which would have been around seven or so. My parents loved movies, and my brother and I followed suit, for many years absorbing whatever was available on the five channels of our black-and-white and then wobbly color TV in Brooklyn in the '60s, and then—still my brother and I—bounding into Manhattan on the D or F trains, to the art cinemas and revival houses in the early and mid-1970s, for many of us a kind of cinematic utopia, temporally, geographically, and historically.

To the point: I grew up a casual cinephile, the way you love things seemingly as a matter of course, and only later are spurred to understand them more deeply: things like family, history, and cinema. Part of my sentimental education was the recognition and appreciation of character actors. This has stayed with me. Character actors frequently have—or at least in the studio system of the Dream Factory had—long careers, careers that tended to follow one of two models: They brought an indelible character with them from film to film, so could make an impression quickly, registering a familiar set of characteristics with the audience simply, after a time, by appearing. Or their essential personality was effaced as they disappeared into each new role. The cast of characters I've written about here, all of whom I have watched since my childhood, follows the limitations of the Dream Factory demographically—it was only after the breakup of the studio system that Hollywood's character base widened in terms of color, fuller possibilities of gender and sexuality, wider and wilder representations of behavior. But that misfortune, too, led to sometimes fascinating "coded" behaviors in the contours of the system of the Code.

Kierkegaard writes that character is "'engraved,' deeply etched." And we sense the character of certain character actors etched into what they carry with them. On the other hand, some character actors blend chameleon-like into a variety of roles, utility performers who step in and can be almost anything needed, repressing their own personalities. In Kierkegaardian terms, they erase, efface. Leading actors also share these templates: Bette Davis could be Queen Victoria or Margo Channing, Charlotte Vale (*Now, Voyager*) or Charlotte Hollis (*Hush, Hush Sweet Charlotte*), a range that would make Gary Cooper cry. Gary Cooper brought a reasonably stable set of characteristics to his roles, which, as

Dorothy Parker said of Katherine Hepburn, "ran the gamut of emotions from A to B."

My interest in character actors might be the same as your interest in the gravediggers, or Rosencrantz and Guildenstern: I grew used to paying attention to them and wondering who they were, elaborating their stories. Have you ever watched a film and just focused on the supporting actors? It's an entirely interesting, if slightly surreal exercise. As a child who felt as though he were destined to play a supporting role, a watching role, I starting looking at how Edward Everett Horton was looking at Fred Astaire, how Mike Mazurki was looking at Tyrone Power, or how, yes, Thelma Ritter was looking at James Stewart. The action, it seemed to me, was on the sidelines. That's where people said more interesting things (character actors could be given lines that evaded the Code, the strict regulating of Hollywood's moral and political presentations in film by the Hayes Motion Picture Code, starting in 1934) simply because less attention was paid to what they said and did. You, meaning I, learned this if you watched closely enough. Did she/he really say that? Did Eve Arden really get away with that? It made character actors intimately and ultimately more interesting to me.

So these essays are my homage, and my attempt to dive under the surface of my long love of character actors. Character actors play with our sense of not just what *a character* is but what *character* is: what defines individual nature, what qualities create a persona, and how demonstrable or latent, how closely guarded the inner life can be. All questions that interest me. And I hope you, enough so that perhaps you're tempted to watch Thelma Ritter, with her greatest of cinematic New York accents.

CELESTE HOLM SYNDROME

1. William Demarest. New York Public Library Digital Collections, Billy Rose Theatre Collection.

2. Esther Hoaward. TCD/Prod.DB / Alamixy Stock Photo.

3. Alan Bridge in *The Miracle of Morgan's Creek* (1944), with Betty Hutton and Diana Lynn.

ON CHARACTERS
PRESTON STURGES'S ENSEMBLE

Preston Sturges's films are a feast of character acting. That isn't to say that some of his films aren't carried by extraordinary lead performances: Henry Fonda and Barbara Stanwyck in *The Lady Eve*; Joel McCrea and, to a lesser degree, Veronica Lake in *Sullivan's Travels*; McCrea, again, and Claudette Colbert in *The Palm Beach Story*. But most of my favorite "lead" performances in his films are still character actors stepping up: Brian Donlevy in *The Great McGinty*; Eddie Bracken and Betty Hutton (her first lead) in *Miracle of Morgan's Creek*; Bracken, again, in *Hail the Conquering Hero*; an underrated Harold Lloyd in her attempted comeback in *Mad Wednesday* (*The Sin of Harold Diddlebock*). Perhaps no other director sustained so vivid a gallery of character actors from film to film: Akim Tamiroff, William Demarest, Julius Tannen, Jimmy Conlin, Byron Foulger, Esther Howard, Emory Parnell, Jack Norton, and others. Paramount objected to Sturges using the same actors over and over again, but Sturges refused to stop using them. He said, "These little players who had contributed so much to my first hits had a moral right to work in my subsequent pictures." Morally courageous and praiseworthy, but I suspect he liked their work, their distinct physiognomies and memorable voices; they're among the best comic character actors ever. If you take a gander at their bios, you'll see that actor after actor appeared in 150 or 200 films. The essence of a character actor is being able to do a lot with a little: maximize time. And these are clearly men and women who, over and over, were used for sometimes little more than moments because the moments became indelible with their voices, mannerisms, faces, with their ability to be more than a face in the crowd. Occasionally—and I'm not talking about Sturges here—a character actor's moment, the indelible aside, two seconds of celluloid, will be worth more than an entire film. This is the link between character and character actors that great directors of secondary actors understand: they also serve who stand and wait for their moment. Think of it this way: have you been on the bus, the subway, on the street, passing the stolid faces, some of them wildly attractive or merely passively pleasant, and you catch sight of the animated eyes, face, who has seen the same absurd sight as you, the anomaly, the weird concordance—he or she rolls her eyes, screws her face into an expression of silly *what do you think of that* solidarity that makes you laugh, an amateur performance? That fragment of character acting stays with you all day, beyond anything else you might have seen: that moment of compressed character.

In *The Great McGinty*—an underestimated Sturges—Esther Howard has a wonderful three-minute scene early on with Brian Donlevy before she disappears. She plays a fortune-teller he has come to shake down for money he owes the boss (Akim Tamiroff, in perhaps his most memorable role). Donlevy explains that paying protection money to one person is a service because it stops the bevy of other shakedowns from the fire department, sanitary department, police department, all of whom would come knocking. Esther Howard is not only convinced by the smooth-talking Donlevy but enamored, and she manages just the right suggestion of dissolution and good-natured tawdriness in inviting him upstairs and telling him that it's a standing invitation. She's much older and is a woman who has, shall we say, been parlaying her own racket: fortune telling, in her classic loose gowns and instrumental use of money and a person's weak spots, just as any hustler does, so she knows that on some level there isn't much use in moral outrage. This Howard conveys in the surrender of her position in wilting voice that is a good-natured concession. Her voice, sagging Boston-accented, and saucer eyes are completely memorable, like Binnie Barnes hard on her luck. She played many such characters—her brief turn in *Murder, My Sweet* (1945), by Edward Dmytryk, must rate a spot in the floozy pantheon—and could convey their histories with a few words. That is the virtue of a character actor: they've been there before, and the histories of their roles come with them. Howard's version of character always adds a strong sense of lived history to her brief turns as women on the downslope of life.

William Demarest has long been a favorite of mine and should be enshrined in the character actor Hall of Fame. Alas, many baby boomers remember him, perhaps, only for the end of career turn he took as Uncle Charlie in *My Three Sons*, which I watched, too. This entry in the homogenized, life-is-good American sitcom of the late 1950s to mid-1960s featured Demarest as the uncle-nanny to the household of a bachelor-widow father, who was all knowing and all-good, played by Fred MacMurray, raising, you guessed it, his three sons. At this point in career and life Demarest's character turn as the man who is crusty, rude, a bit crude, talks to himself, and works as a kind of engineer for another man to get things done, had gotten too old and tired, which is to say, Demarest had. It was as though the vinegar, the comically tonic function of Demarest's earlier roles in *The Lady Eve*; *Christmas in July*; *Hail the Conquering Hero*; *Miracle of Morgan's Creek*; *The Palm Beach Story*; *Sullivan's Travels*; and *The Great Moment*—all of Preston Sturges's great films—along with 140 other film roles, some in wonderful films like *Mr. Smith Goes to Washington* but mostly in second rate or B movies, had been wrung out, leaving dyspepsia.

Leave it to Sturges to have discovered how centrally American, how wonderfully direct, how perfectly unpretentious a character Demarest could mine for comedy.

Demarest was a great verbal and physical comedian, and his greatest role is *The Miracle of Morgan's Creek* (though he is really superb in all of the Sturges films). In *The Miracle of Morgan's Creek*, he plays Constable Kockenlocker—yes, Kockenlocker—in 1943, although the film wasn't released until 1944. James Agee commented, and please excuse the political incitement, that the Hay's Office censor "must have been raped in his sleep" to have allowed the film to go through. Perhaps the distraction of the war? But then again, the film was subjected to any number of rewrites to be considered acceptable. *The Miracle of Morgan's Creek*, one of the greatest American comedies, is about (and here we get to the absurd and reductionist levels of plot summary) a young woman who tricks the man who loves her so she can borrow his car, winds up pregnant and falsely married to a soldier whose name she can't remember, falls in love with the man she tricked, and gives birth to six babies, fueling the war effort, and all but assuring Hitler's defeat (I told you). Thus James Agee's comment. Her father is played by William Demarest; has there ever been a name that mocked the patriarchy more than Constable Kockenlocker? What would a contemporary audience do with that name? I want to be in a movie theater in Brooklyn, in 1944, so I can listen for the response any time his name is mentioned.

As Constable Kockenlocker, Demarest, whose voice was somewhere between a man's version of an East Side Kid and a goat who had miraculously learned to speak, is constantly trying and failing to control his two daughters, played with anarchic energy of very different kinds by Betty Hutton, who is physical and sexual, a small town volcano, and Diana Lynn, the apotheosis of the smart-alecky and too-smart kid sister. On several occasions Demarest, taunted or driven to distraction by his daughters (several times he says, "Daughters, phooey," even breaking the fourth wall to turn to the camera and announce it—and as an aside, as much as I thought *Fleabag* brilliant in every way, it isn't the breaking of the fourth wall that's inventive: Groucho Marx, Gracie Allen, Bob Hope, other characters in Sturges, etc. break the fourth wall; it's *how* Waller-Bridge uses her turns to the camera to connect to us that's striking), tries to teach them a late lesson with some corporal punishment: kicking them, swatting them, and so on. It always ends with him on his ass, or worse for wear. When Demarest—Kockenlocker—tries to pummel Norbert, played as the ultimate schlemiel by Eddie Bracken, the father's two daughters jump him and disable him. This is what happens when the Kockenlocker patriarchy is taken on by women. The brilliance of William Demarest, what makes him indelible, is his quality of blowhard aggressive masculinity with just enough vulnerability, enough actual concern for his daughters in *Morgan's Creek*, to allow us to find him funny, endearing actually, and not offensive or threatening. Demarest undermines, in other words, his own masculinity through a kind of innate understanding of hyperbole. That's his brilliance. He always plays a kind of operator, a guy who is trying to force things, a guy who thinks he knows the ropes. But Demarest knows how to hesitate just enough in his aggression so that it's denatured, reversed, even benignant at times.

Another thing: in repose, he can look a little like an older, slightly heavier Buster Keaton crossed with a bit of bulldog. But unlike the "great stone face," Demarest tends to scowl. He has a Mack Sennett tendency to do double takes, rub his face, and turn to the camera when he's frustrated, which is frequent. Demarest is the muse of frustration, the man of bluster who ends up with egg on his face. That's why his Kockenlocker is so iconic, such an absurd, central, and shocking deconstruction of American manhood: he's the figure of authority, the head of the family, the man who directs traffic, the war veteran, and he gets everything wrong, his daughters' mock and elude him, the new generation of soldiers (World War II) teases him, he's impotent, thus: Kockenlocker. And Demarest manages this meltdown with, at first, the indignity of someone who thinks he should be empowered but is instead a joke, and who then becomes ennobled by, if not a full, at least an instrumental sense of his own limits. As the film progresses, Demarest allows his bluster (derived from the Low German *blüstren*, to blow violently, in other words, the same source as "blow," most likely, which becomes in the mid-fifteenth century on a weather-related term, the blowing of winds, and probably in the sixteenth century in English, the violent blowing of winds) to soften; his rough gales becoming something closer to a kind of weathered grace in the face of what his daughter and her endlessly sacrificing beau have gone through. It's quite moving.

Perhaps this is the reason Demarest was frequently cast comically in caretaker roles. In *The Great McGinty* he's the all-purpose political hack who runs interference for the political novice. In *Hail the Conquering Hero* his attempt to take care of Eddie Bracken backfires, and Demarest, with the subtlety of a ground attack, moves in at the end to save him from the folds of lies and deceptions that have been forced on him.

Demarest was always good with a line to reprise (character actors, after all, are frequently careers built on the idea of reprise, variations on the theme of a memorable look, delivery); in *Miracle of Morgan's Creek* it's "Daughter's, phooey," and in *The Lady Eve* his tagline is a variation of "The same dame!"—as Barbara Stanwyck unwinds her elaborate plan to play her own double and fool Henry Fonda, for whom Demarest acts as companion-bodyguard. Demarest's everyman quality, a quality many of the greatest character actors put across (they seem somehow recognizable, not unreachably beautiful, or glamorous, or fascinating like Marilyn Monroe, or Ronald Colman, or Fred Astaire), serves Sturges well as, with his indecorous slang and midwestern accent, he punctures any moment where decorum threatens to establish itself. More often than not, to mix metaphors, he's a bull in a china shop who thinks he smells a rat—suspicious to his core but also devoted to protecting those under his care. That's why we like him. He's the emblem of those we excuse because their motives are pure.

Demarest gets the last word in *The Lady Eve*, and it's a line, a moment worthy of the best Billy Wilder closers (he had the best last lines). Demarest, who has been spying on Barbara Stanwyck—protective as he is of Henry Fonda, his smart but feckless charge—has been in wait in Fonda's shipboard cabin. And as Stanwyck and Fonda extravagantly exchange vows of love, and as Stanwyck attempts unsuccessfully to explain to Fonda the nature of the almost-Shakespearean play of masquerade (actually an inversion of disguise, a kind of challenge to cognitive dissonance, as Barbara Stanwyck disappears, then appears to assert a new identity) that has taken place, they slip into the room and close the door. At which point Demarest, having been in the room with the two lovers, opens the door, gently closes it, and turns toward the camera: "Positively the same dame," he says. This is a line he has been saying throughout the second half of the film—challenging both the beau monde's and nouveau riche's enchantment with Stanwyck's impersonation of an aristocratic Englishwoman. He's sure she's the brash young American he suspected of trying to cheat his naïve heir, Fonda. But what's so brilliant about his performance is that he seems just a shade less than positive. The ruse has been that thorough and complicated. And at this point, he's willing, as fairy godfather, to leave the lovers be, though in this fairyland, nothing can ever be taken for granted.

Gruff and frequently mistaken though he is, barking, loud Demarest almost always plays a character who is loyal. Perhaps Sturges could tell that was just in his character.

In the Sturges universe, Alan Bridge defines the obverse of the William Demarest type of character actor who brings similar traits from role to role. Bridge, who appeared in small roles in an astonishing number of films—over 250—appeared in 10 Sturges films but had crucially different roles in *Sullivan's Travels* and *Miracle of Morgan's Creek*. In the former he played a cruel prison warden, a sadist who seemed to enjoy torture; in the latter, he heartbreakingly defines discretion and empathy, with a slight note of 1940s patriarchal disapproval, still striking for the time.

In *Sullivan's Travels* (1941)—perhaps the most lionized Preston Sturges film—Joel McCrea, a wealthy Hollywood director of popular, silly comedies, is bothered by what seems the unseriousness of his endeavor during the Depression and wants to make a statement, direct a film of what he considers artistic merit. But to do so he needs experience of the underclass and their suffering, and so he, with Veronica Lake in tow, goes undercover as a hobo to attempt to do the research for the film that will be *Oh, Brother Where Art Thou*. (Yes, the Coen brothers are enormous fans of, and in many ways imitators of, Preston Sturges.) Suffice to say, the plot twists in a screwball way, and McCrea's Sullivan ends up with amnesia in a prison labor camp, a version of a chain gang, doing hard time for manslaughter. His warden is Alan Bridge, whose boss-warden role is ominously billed as "The Mister." In other words: "The Man." It's the comic prefiguring of *Hud*.

Alan Bridge had a remarkable voice, and voice is one of the qualities we associate most with notable character actors, since an unusual aural impression (Billie Burke! "Are you a good witch or a bad witch?" Christopher Walken! "This watch is your birthright.") is as crucial to the creation of cinematic character as visage. The character actors who became leads almost all had indelible voices: James Cagney, Edward G. Robinson, Dustin Hoffman, Walter Matthau, Judy Holliday, Alastair Sim. Voice is so hard to describe without referring to other voices—it's all metaphor. Bridge's voice was middle range, that place between baritone and tenor, and his accent equally escapable, somewhere on the border between Midwest and West, with vowels trailing off high; it was the Plains, with a touch of Badlands, some rain turning to snow in the foothills. There was another quality to his voice—not quite guttural, but as though the sounds were being slightly squeezed, the words forced out because of some undefined difficulty. This could make him sound reticent and sympathetic, as in *Morgan's Creek*, or menacing, as in *Sullivan's Travels*.

In *Sullivan's Travels* this reticence conveys an utter lack of sympathy as he threatens and then orders Sullivan—Joel McCrea—beaten. His voice seems expressionless. Something or someone took everything out of him, and that flint in the accent suggests it has to do with place.

In *Morgan's Creek*, Bridge plays a lawyer whom Betty Hutton (Trudy) and Diana Lynn (as her sister, Emmy) seek out in desperation when they learn that Trudy is pregnant. It's an extraordinary scene—I don't know of another like it in '40s cinema, in which an older man is being called on to weigh in on what was then a woman's moral transgression that baffles him, and whose circumstances are bizarre. (Remember, Trudy doesn't remember the circumstances of her pregnancy or the soldier she supposedly married.) Trudy and Emmy try, rather transparently, to ask Mr. Johnson (Bridge), a lawyer, what "their friend" should do in this hypothetically disastrous case. Bridge, who stands and paces, responds with impatient sympathy, which, given the times and the situation, seems . . . deeply, humanly responsive in Alan Bridge's performance. He begins rather severely, disposing of his paternal obligation to disapprove by saying, "Your friend ought to be ashamed of herself. . . . I mean because of her carelessness." (Emmy, not to let this by, says, "She's a very nice girl. It just happened. That's all.") However, he goes on, hilariously, to indicate his helplessness (the men, in this wartime film, are largely clueless, castrated, or inept, with the exception of the absent "husband" of Trudy): "Your friend doesn't remember the bridegroom's name? And she used an assumed name. Perfect. That's really airtight." The women ask if the marriage could be annulled, or the man divorced or sued for alimony, and Bridge says, "Sue who, annul who? Look, I practice the law. I'm not only willing but anxious to sue anyone anytime for anything. But they've got to be real people with names and corpuses and meat on their bones. I can't work with spooks. Your friend doesn't need a lawyer, she needs a medium." It's an intensely exasperated response, but slightly leavened by the comic impulse. And then comes the switch. He says their fee is five dollars, which they should use to buy flowers for their friend on "the happy day." When they ask if he'll tell anyone, he says, "How can I, when I don't even know who she is?" They leave, and Bridge turns with a look of ultimate paternalistic concern, simply troubled for the young woman's plight. It's a memorable minute and thirty-three seconds (yes, a minute and a half). But Alan Bridge's Mr. Johnson has stayed with me for forty years—that voice of umbrage shading into melancholy sympathy. He uses his briefest of appearances as a character actor to memorialize the generationally encumbered parental figure, who still manages to be a human being in the face of someone's pain. Sturges understood the impact that a character actor could have in a fleeting scene.

I could write about all Sturges's character actors, but then, I feel I could write about so many character actors. Why? Because they made me see something out of the corner of my eye, and what I saw made me feel different(ly) or think about something I hadn't thought of before. Character actors are more like us because they aren't demigods, the lead actors, and also unlike us in that they're frequently so unusual, so unique: "You're such a character," we say to someone who stands out, who's different in some exaggerated way. We like to think we're such characters, too (don't we? Or do I overgeneralize here? I like to think I am. That I register as different, perhaps even strange, not in an unpleasant way but rather in an interesting way) that's why we like them. But we—all right, or *I*—are really the less exaggerated versions of the types and the idiosyncratic individuals in the characters actors' repertoire.

Because they aren't center stage, there is a modesty to the character actor: even the hammiest, most over the top, schtick-fest character actor is usually not in the center ring, or not for long. The loneliness of the long distance character actor: they watch the leads, and I love to watch them watch, perform their tricks, recede, but not from memory, at least not mine. What magic, to suggest human dimensionality on a flat screen in just a few minutes. What humility mixed with persistent faith, to think that these occasional moments of impersonation, these brief acted lives on the margins of narrative, could really matter to those of us sitting out there in the dark, ensembles of one.

4. Oscar Wilde. New York Public Library Digital Collections, Billy Rose Theatre Collection.

5. Oscar Levant. © age fotostock.

MY TWO OSCARS

ON WIT AND MELANCHOLY

ROSALIND: They say you are a melancholy fellow.
JACQUES: I am so; I do love it better than laughing.

—*As You Like It*

Underneath this flabby exterior is an enormous lack of character.

—Oscar Levant, *An American in Paris*

Oscar Levant is a melancholy figure, full of barbed wit, self-loathing, and "Rhapsody in Blue," which he performed more than any other twentieth-century pianist. You may not know who he is, though Jack Paar used to go off the air after a time saying, "Goodnight Oscar Levant, wherever you are." Jimmy Durante used to say, "Goodnight Mrs. Calabash, wherever you are," and no one ever knew who she was, which he must have found disconcerting.

Oscar Wilde, you undoubtedly know, but you may think of him staring languidly into the camera, dressed as a dandy, self-pleased.

I think of my two Oscars as trying to say the perfectly witty thing as a way of staying the melancholy that dare not speak its name. I think of wit as a stay against melancholy, a brief moment of verbal perfection, before its self-immolation: time.

Our attitude toward wit is: what have you said for me lately?

Wits, whether Dorothy Parker or Oscar Levant (friends, by the way), or Oscar Wilde, or Samuel Johnson, make their own traps that wit springs them out of: expectation. The only way a wit can stop being a wit is to be dull, a melancholy resolution.

Oscar Levant looked a bit like a cross between Leslie Caron and Delmore Schwartz on a bad day, except for his long fingers, which must have played "Rhapsody in Blue" a thousand times. If you don't know who Leslie Caron and Delmore Schwartz are, let's say Levant looked like a moon for the misbegotten, with bad teeth. So, early in the essay I keep asking if you know who people are—that really means I'm concerned about my age, and yours, about whether this is a December-May essay, which might be a melancholy affair.

Like Leslie Caron, with whom he starred in *An American in Paris*, when he was known as one of the wittiest men in America, Levant had moony eyes. This was before he spiraled into multiple psychiatric commitments, addiction, and electric shock therapy. He would emerge one of the wittiest broken men in America, and the first full-fledged American performative psychodrama: he prefigured reality TV and the performance comedy of the neurotic self in actor comedians like Woody Allen, Larry David, and Louis C.K. "What do you do for exercise?" Jack Paar asked him in 1959. "I stumble and fall into a coma," Levant said. That, of course, would relieve him of his wits (the Old English *gewitt*, the base of consciousness). If melancholy, not brevity, is the soul of wit, perhaps it is because sadness is our natural fallen state. Awareness is a painful condition: moony, misbegotten, sublunary—except when Oscar played the piano.

Melancholia, you may already know, derives from the

Greek (which seems rather perfect to me; one person's epic hero is another's sad, anxious wanderer, or monomaniacal and impulsive oppositional type with authority problems) *melaina chole*, translated into Latin as *astra billis* and English as the black bile, an excess of which caused, and perhaps still causes for all we know, chronic sadness, which is, according to Hippocrates, in the fifth century BCE, one of the four humors, or temperaments, along with the Sanguine, the Choleric, and the Phlegmatic.

Aristotle, as far as we know, wrote the first essay on melancholy, at the least, the first that survives. And the temperaments are still being tossed around in the twentieth and twenty-first century: Balanchine and Hindemith collaborated on *The Four Temperaments*, Carl Nielsen composed a symphony called the *Four Temperaments*, the Waldorf schools rely on a version of them in their pedagogical ideology (so if you have melancholy children, relax, you know where to enroll them), and so on. Seneca, in *De tranquillitate animi*, notes the difficulty of pinning down melancholy, or violent sadness, in name or cause. Burton, temperamentally rather different than Seneca, eases melancholy by musing over just this difficulty for hundreds of pages, to our delight.

The Hippocratic, or Temperamental school of thought, merged or married with the Latin in the form of Galen in the second century, and melancholy began its slow dance between this condition as problem and irremediable burden, or mark of specialness, even genius, as the melancholic looks inward, acts different, perhaps even performs a Saint Vitus dance of the self, and is possessed of some inordinate talent. In his journals, published as *Straw for the Fire*, Theodore Roethke writes, "Sure I'm crazy. But it ain't easy." In *Anatomy of Melancholy*, Burton writes, "Why melancholy men are witty, which Aristotle hath long since maintained in his Problems, and that all learned men, famous philosophers, and lawgivers, *ad unum fere omnes melancholici*, have still been melancholy, is a problem much controverted." Burton also refers to the Aristotelian or pseudo-Aristotle *Problema* of the fourth century BCE—so the idea had melancholy legs.

As Clark Lawlor notes, in *From Melancholia to Prozac*, "The Renaissance saw the rise of the first form of melancholy in a flourishing of the myth of melancholic genius that has persisted up to the present day" (42). Marsilio Ficino, the fifteenth-century philosopher priest, aided the union of melancholy and genius, sprinkling the discourse of love and alchemy, and finding that, in fact, every man of genius was melancholic, though the humoral conception of the body maintains, as we see in Montaigne.

In his *Letters on the Aesthetic Education of Man* (1795), Schiller avers that we all share in the condition of melancholia. Perhaps that's the real beginning of the history of "depression." Attention must be paid when melancholy separates from genius and becomes ordinary.

In the nineteenth century, melancholy becomes pharmaceutical, at least in a more organized way with the spreading use of opium, laudanum, which had been around since Thomas Sydenham, "the English Hippocrates," concocted it in the seventeenth century. His recipe: opium, two ounces; saffron, one ounce; bruised cinnamon and bruised cloves, each one drachm; sherry wine, one pint. Mix and macerate for fifteen days and filter. Twenty drops are equal to one grain of opium. The results, as we know, thrilling and disastrous.

Not every melancholic is a genius. But Oscar Levant, along

with his namesake Oscar Wilde, was a self-made genius, at least a self-proclaimed one, which alternated with a deep vein of self-laceration, a running theme of his witticisms. At the beginning of *An American in Paris*, Levant, who wrote almost all the lines for the films he was in, announces, "I'm the world's oldest child prodigy." Self-pity and delusions of grandeur—a classic combination! Except that Levant was an excellent concert pianist.

I'm not sure if any of us quite know what a genius is. But Levant did: it was George Gershwin, and he measured himself against Gershwin disastrously.

How melancholy to become the memorialist for the man you loved ("The Man I Love"?) and against whom you measured yourself so severely.

All of Levant's film performances, from *Romance on the High Seas* to *Humoresque* to *The Barkleys of Broadway* to *An American in Paris*, are variations on the theme of Oscar Levant, the amanuensis of love, the musical third wheel. Oscar is always there to help speed or console the romantic action. But along the way, he gives us bracing asides; he'll tell us that "my psychiatrist once said to me, 'Maybe life isn't for everyone.'" He's the tonic to the saccharine action.

Oscar Levant said, repeatedly, "There is a fine line between genius and insanity. I have erased that line." It reminds me of the line in Montaigne's "Of Cripples": "I have seen no more evident monstrosity and miracle in the world than myself." If there is a kind of theory of melancholy in Montaigne's essays, a melancholy apologia, it's in "Of Democritus and Heraclitus." He writes:

Democritus and Heraclitus were two philosophers, of whom the first, finding the condition of man vain and ridiculous, never went out in public but with a mocking and laughing face; whereas Heraclitus, having pity and compassion on this same condition of ours, wore a face perpetually sad, and eyes filled with tears. I prefer the first humor; not because it is pleasanter to laugh than to weep, but because it is more disdainful, and condemns us more than the other; and it seems to me that we can never be despised as much as we deserve. Pity and commiseration are mingled with some esteem for the thing we pity; the things we laugh at we consider worthless. I do not think there is as much unhappiness in us as vanity, nor as much malice as stupidity. We are not so full of evil as of inanity; we are not as wretched as we are worthless.

Oscar Levant veers between Democritian and Heraclitian melancholy, tending toward the former. Consider: "There used to be an act in the old Club Eighteen in New York where a temporarily unemployed actor would step into a green spotlight in the middle of the floor and commence to recite Longfellow's poem which begins: 'I shot an arrow into the air. It fell to earth I knew not where.' The reciter would pause, then sadly say: 'I lose more damned arrows that way.' That has been my history of manufacturing jocose remarks" (*The Unimportance of Being Oscar*, 15).

Oscar Levant told this story obsessively: George Gershwin and Levant were taking the train together, spending the night in the Pullman, and Gershwin swung into the lower bunk. As Levant was climbing into the top bunk, Gershwin said, "You see Oscar, that's the difference between genius and talent. Lower bunk, top bunk." Ironically, in *Rhapsody in Blue*, Levant himself speaks the line, making the distinction. Is this deference to Gershwin, or self-slight, post-mortem? It isn't completely clear if the two friends had been playfully sparring, or if Gershwin was sadistically poking Levant. He seemed to like to keep Levant in his place, to let him know who the real genius was. After asking Levant to perform with him at Lewisohn Stadium, Gershwin asked Levant if he wanted to be paid or have a watch that Gershwin had inscribed for him: "To Oscar, from George." For the next thirty-five years Levant never performed without wearing it.

Levant met Gershwin when both were reasonably young, but Gershwin was already being touted as the next big thing and would become it. Levant would become a hanger-on, a Gershwin interpreter, interloper, intimate—apparently anything with an *i*, as long as it didn't distract from Gershwin's ego. Levant became so associated with "Rhapsody in Blue" that there are references to it in all his films. Those are Levant's hands playing the piano for Robert Alda in the piano sequences in the Gershwin biopic *Rhapsody in Blue*, and Levant plays "Rhapsody in Blue" in its entirety in the film.

Having established himself as the sidekick to Gershwin, Oscar Levant played a sidekick in his films. But he was a different take on the sidekick—isolate, never fawning, the self-possessed neurotic, if that isn't a contradiction in terms. You keep expecting Levant to break the fourth wall, the way Groucho does in the Marx Brothers movies. In *Rhythm on the River*, with Bing Crosby and Mary Martin, Levant is lounging, reading his own memoir, *A Smattering of Ignorance*. "A very irritating book," he comments before putting it down. Frequently, Oscar Levant mutters something brilliant out of range of anyone but us, which establishes, with fierce economy, our relationship with him and the very nature of most wit: it's actually unheard. "I find that girl completely resistible," he says to himself in *The Barkleys of Broadway*. In *Humoresque*, he mutters, "I envy people who drink. At least they know what to blame everything on."

An American in Paris (1951) may be Oscar Levant's most well-known film role, partly because it's his most well-known film, even a notch more than *The Band Wagon* (1953), a much better film. The two films are separated by two years, two dancers, and a heart attack—Oscar's. The dancers are Gene Kelly and Fred Astaire. I must admit a prejudice against *An American in Paris*, the second Gershwin-inspired film Levant is featured in. Here it is: Despite being an avowed Fred Astaire acolyte, I've liked Gene Kelly pretty well in most of his major films. But not here. His character, Jerry Mulligan (named after Gerry Mulligan? The saxophone player that moved to Los Angeles after leaving Miles Davis's band) is a struggling artist who is taken up by the beautiful and sexually available socialite Milo Roberts, played by Nina Foch. Because of his fear of being sexually and financially castrated by Milo, Jerry ends up repeatedly sexually humiliating her in his pursuit of the gamin Lise Bouvier, played by Leslie Caron. (Levant looked like Caron in a funhouse mirror, like her father once removed by disaster.) Gene Kelly's Jerry Mulligan paintings are awful, warmed-over street corner impressionism, and his character superficial, casually cruel, and narcissistic. So here's this nice looking wannabe artist, whom this enchanting woman does everything for (sure, he dances reasonably well, a nice smile), but I think Nina Foch is enchanting: supportive, witty, abandoned. Is there a specific neurosis to our objection to the fates of characters central to the rhythm of films of novels, whose disposition we find objectionable? My Nina Foch objection (which I'll talk about again later, like any good obsession), which I experience like righteous indignation, has been my central pleasure in watching the film, a film I don't love. It's an experience of neurotic movie watching that Levant would probably appreciate. In the film, Foch's original sin is that she's older and richer than Gene Kelly. Yes, "I Got Rhythm" is a charming number, but the film leaves a bad taste in my mouth. Structurally, there is a strange moment at the very beginning where we're almost offered a narrative alternative. We see the life of Jerry Mulligan, struggling artist, genius manqué. And then we're presented with Adam Cook, Oscar Levant, the nascent concert pianist, the real artist. But we don't ultimately get parallel narratives, which would be the interesting film that we don't get to go back and shoot. Oscar is the narrative not taken. We see Cook's talent whenever Levant sits at the piano.

He's playing Gershwin, of course.

Oscar Levant tries to mediate his two friends' interest in the same woman in the film, but it just makes him a nervous wreck: the wreck of the Levant, which sounds like a great disaster. It was, eventually. However, in one of the most fully realized sequences of Levant's film career, he fantasizes playing Gershwin's "Concerto in F," and conducting, and playing the violin, and being in the audience—simultaneously. It's a sly and funny commentary, dreamed up by Levant, who pitched it to Vincente Minnelli, about ambition, artistic ego, self-congratulation, and at the end of the fantasia Levant is back in melancholy real time, shaking his head as though to say, "Well, yeah, in my dreams"—the real work of the performing artist.

Oscar Levant provides us with an alternative, if unde-veloped, possibility of character in the film: he doesn't care about money at all. He may fantasize, but he doesn't sell out or throw anyone under an emotional bus. "The supreme vice is shallowness," as Wilde writes in *De Profundis*. Levant is our alternative to Kelly's shallowness in *American in Paris*.

"I'm a concert pianist," he says. "That's a pretentious way of saying I'm unemployed at the moment."

The melancholy of wit is frequently accompanied by unre-quited love, the wit turned inward as if saying *this is what I should have expected*, or what I deserve. Dorothy Parker's "I am Marie of Romania" and her line about an early abortion: "That's what I get for putting all my eggs in one bastard." Levant was enthralled with Gershwin, call it what you will.

Oscar Levant was completely aware of his namesake, the other Oscar, Wilde, whose unrequited love is the occasion of his most melancholy, penultimate work, *De Profundis*. Levant calls his ultimate memoir *The Unimportance of Being Oscar*. In the 1955 film *The Cobweb*, Levant, severely diminished by having been a mental patient so often the last several years, is undergoing hydrotherapy. A nurse stops in to tell him it's time for bed. Levant, who wrote almost all of his own lines, says, "That's the wittiest thing anyone has said since Oscar Wilde." And in *The Unimportance of Being Oscar*, Levant writes, "The two great writers who have never let me down over years are Samuel Johnson and Oscar Wilde" (174).

In "The Critic as Artist" (1888) Oscar Wilde writes, "What people call insincerity is simply a method by which we can multiply our personalities." He also says, in self-enshrinement, "It is much more difficult to talk about a thing than to do it." There is a melancholy vein in Wilde—in this essay as elsewhere—that fully emerges only after his fall in *De Profundis*. But even earlier, when he speaks of music in "The Critic as Artist," Wilde writes, "After playing Chopin, I feel as if I had been weeping over sins that I had never committed, and mourning over tragedies that were not my own."

Reading *De Profundis* is always a profoundly moving and strange experience. It's one of the most wrenching works of epistolary literature. Wilde can't seem to break free of Alfred Douglas, Bosie as he calls him, despite compiling a rogue's gallery of offenses that Bosie has committed against him, really nasty stuff, like when he left Wilde alone in his rooms in Paris when he was dreadfully ill, despite Wilde's having cared for Bosie during *his* illness. The line that Wilde can't shake is Bosie having said to him, "When you are not on your pedestal, you are not interesting." When Wilde was ill, he was not on his pedestal, not interesting, but there for Bosie to tap into for cash. Wilde's refrain in *De Profundis* is, "The supreme vice is shallowness." He repeats it like an accusation, but it's a self-haunting line. Nothing is shallower than the flat surface of a mirror.

In "Mourning and Melancholia" Freud distinguishes between the conscious grief one feels at the loss of a loved one through death, and the loss of a beloved object we have desired and identified with, which puts us in an unconscious state of grieving, of melancholia. Freud stresses that the melancholic has "a loss in regard to his ego." He goes on to explain the nature of the loss, the transformation, the internalizing of the other: "The shadow of the object fell upon the ego, and the latter could henceforth be judged by a special agency, as though it were an object, the forsaken object. In this way an object-loss was transformed into an ego-loss." The melancholic in this vision has become the thing he has lost, and he con-tinually loses himself. For this to happen, "a strong fixation to the loved object must have been present." I think of Oscar Levant's melancholy devotion to George Gershwin. "If it wasn't for George Gershwin I could have been a pretty good mediocre composer," he said.

With Lord Alfred Douglas and George Gershwin, Wilde and Levant found complex and troubling mirrors in which they both could and couldn't see their *own* reflections:

> I could have held up a mirror to you, and shown you such an image of yourself that you would not have recognized. (*De Profundis*, 37)

> An evening with George Gershwin is a George Gershwin evening. (Levant, various sources)

> The memory of our friendship is the shadow that walks with me here. (*De Profundis*, 29)

> Tell me, George, if you had it to do all over, would you fall in love with yourself again? (Levant)

The shadow of the other, the other's self-love, the love of the self-love of the other: it's a melancholy train of association and dissociation. Levant said, "It's not what you are, it's what you don't become that hurts." Wilde echoes this in *De Profundis*: "I ruined myself and . . . nobody, great or small, can be ruined, except by his own hand." But both men veer between a tragic sense of responsibility for having not lived up to potential and a longing, angry gaze at the other who impeded them, who led them down the path to self-disgust, failure.

Oscar Levant was extraordinarily homophobic—he admits as much in *Memoirs of an Amnesiac*, his second memoir—and Gershwin was . . . a mystery, gay, bisexual, confused? It's still not clear. In *Memoirs of an Amnesiac*, Levant writes, "Spender had written a rather shocking, revelatory autobiography dealing in some part with homosexuality, and I said to Isherwood [who was and remained a dear friend], 'I know that Spender's half Jewish. Does that account for it?" Does that account for Levant's half-acknowledged love for Gershwin? He writes: "I was often lightheartedly acrimonious or sarcastic with him, but my real feeling for him was undiluted idolatry." One wonders if Gershwin was interesting off his pedestal, if he ever was.

Levant's forbidding and distant father died when he was fourteen. His mother seemed to care most about his success at the piano, and at fifteen dropped him off alone in New York from their home in Pittsburgh so he could take lessons and make his way. Levant relates the story of his father sitting him down on Saturday night, his "night for chastisement," and telling him the following story:

> A son murders his mother and cuts her heart out to present to his sweetheart. With the heart in his hand he rushes off to present it to his fiancée. In his hurry he stumbles, and the disembodied heart that he clutches in his hand cries out, "Did you hurt yourself son?"

Levant says the story made him feel "free and easy." Which part?

As much as I love Oscar Levant's melancholic pith, his fuck-it-all daring on the air—"I said outrageous things that not only frightened me, but the whole community," he writes in *Memoirs of an Amnesiac*—I think what startled me into caring more about him was that after years of going in and out of Mount Sinai for addiction, clinical depression, shock therapy, he encountered a fellow patient, an old man, who was disconsolate at being prevented from seeing his son and began to cry. Levant put his arm around him and said, "Suddenly I forgot all my troubles. . . . I'd let go of myself" (*Amnesiac*). He experienced real empathy for the first time, and knew it. He was fifty.

In 1945, six years after Gershwin's stunning death from a brain tumor, Jesse L. Lasky decided to produce the Gershwin biopic *Rhapsody in Blue*. It is a really awful film. If you've read anything about Gershwin, you know he had a kind of charismatic reserve, watchfulness, and self-involvement. Robert Alda's lovesick musical enthusiast, now vacuously narcissistic, now vivacious in his ingenuous outpouring of talent, is hard to stomach. The musical numbers aren't even particularly well staged, for the most part (though it's always grand to see Jolson—he seems very excited and does a sweet bit of two stepping, and Anne Brown is marvelous singing "Summertime"). Levant was the musical adviser for the film and played the piano parts that Alda mimicked. Most strangely, of all his roles—usually a melancholy version of himself, writing his own lines—here Levant actually plays himself, Oscar Levant, Gershwin friend and hanger-on, re-creating the lines he did say, or might have said, or *l'espirit del'escalier*, wished he had said. As in most of his films, Levant almost seems like an interloper: he doesn't really act, he seems to have just wandered on from off set, or as if someone said, let's get Oscar Levant in this scene to liven it up with a few good lines. But he is more comfortable here, in this biopic rotten egg, than in most of his other films, more relaxed, as though playing Oscar

Levant to George Gershwin were the role he *had* to perform, or perhaps that he was just doing a pantomime of real life. But if you watch it, you can trace the slight amusement in his temper. Is it because Gershwin is alive *and* dead? (The live Gershwin, for once, doesn't outshine him?)

Every time a number is performed, the camera cuts to Gershwin's greenhorn father announcing: five minutes, twelve minutes; his son's coming up in the theater world measured by how much time he is taking up on stage. One winces. But consider: *Rhapsody in Blue* was directed by Irving Rapper, who directed *Marjorie Morningstar*, *Now Voyager*, and *The Christine Jorgensen Story*. Levant ends up being the star of *Rhapsody in Blue* by default, playing the music, speaking the best lines. True, a slightly desultory achievement in a lousy film, but a film, nevertheless, that was given an enormous sendoff by Warner Brothers. Remarkably, in the last scene of the film, after Gershwin's death, as Levant plays "Rhapsody in Blue" at the Lewisohn Stadium memorial concert, we see the Gershwin faux-love interest (Joan Leslie) watch Levant turn into Gershwin. What a stunning wish fulfillment for Levant!

Freud writes, again in "Mourning and Melancholia," that "the occasions which give rise to the illness extend for the most part beyond the clear case of a loss by death, and include all those situations of being slighted, neglected or disappointed, which can import opposed feelings of love and hate into the relationship or reinforce an already existing ambivalence." But what about when there is both, both mourning and melancholia, both death and neglect? I suppose the answer would be, rather obviously, mourning and melancholia.

The irony of this is that Levant had far from an undistinguished career. He was in thirteen films, including *An*

American in Paris, Humoresque, The Band Wagon; he was a radio phenomenon for several years on *Information Please* in the late '40s, early '50s; he was a popular and classical composer, he toured widely for years with a contemporary and classical repertoire, and was for several years the highest paid pianist in the country; he published three memoirs that sold handsomely; he had a reputation as one of the wittiest men in the country.

And he was one of the first people to expose the fragility of their mental health publicly, going on TV repeatedly, both his own television show and Jack Paar's, to talk about his addictions, his shock therapy, his hypochondria, his general decline in the mid-to-late-'50s. But there had always been a sharp edge to Oscar Levant. It was why people who loved Oscar Levant loved Oscar Levant. He created the persona of the self-aware, self-mocking neurotic, the person in the room who was aware of everything going on in the room but was never the center of attention. He was, in other words, off-center, before off-center became culturally central.

Although he was an extraordinary pianist, accompanying anyone on anything, leading Broadway orchestras, the favorite second piano to Gershwin, later taken on as a student by Schoenberg, it was his wit that got him entry; declared the "wag of Broadway" by Walter Winchell, he hung around with gangsters and the Guggenheims and was one of the best friends of Harpo Marx, the man everybody loved. Women seemed to like him especially, and men with lower levels of testosterone. Hyper-masculine types and the egomaniacal tended to see in his devastating one-liners deflation heading right between their eyes.

He said, "I admire Leonard Bernstein, but not as much as

he does," and, "He uses music as an accompaniment to his conducting."

He said, famously, "I knew Doris Day before she was a virgin."

He said of Eisenhower, "Once he makes up his mind, he's full of indecision."

The line that got him taken off the air, on live television in 1958: "Now that Marilyn Monroe has converted to Judaism, Arthur Miller can eat her."

Of Grace Kelly: "She married the first Prince who asked."

Of himself: "I'm a study of a man in chaos in search of frenzy."

But there was something wounded, something vulnerable in his mien before he became outright self-destructive. That happened right after he filmed *Band Wagon*, in 1953, after his heart attack, when fear of death sent him chasing after it, into Demerol addiction.

In the Middle Ages jesters were kept by kings partly for their ability to entertain, but also because they could be expected to tell the truth, wittily, to utter the unpalatable. This license kept their positions secure. Rahere was the jester to Henry I in the twelfth century. (He later became a cleric and founded St. Bartholomew's Hospital). He was called the "joculator" (which is a wonderful title). But one wonders if the joculators were always so secure. Wit, it seems to me, is always accompanied by the uncertainty of timing, like the goalie's anxiety before the penalty kick, and the exigency of expectation, and it's evil twin, deflation. Imagine Dorothy Parker, expected to deliver the epigram, which Oscar Levant called "a wisecrack that's played Carnegie Hall." Is that what he considered himself? A wisecrack that played Carnegie Hall? Parker came to loathe

the demand that she utter something quotable, some witticism whenever she spoke.

A couple of my favorite lines of Levant's are actually moments when the anxiety peeks through, when the melancholy nature of wit, the charge of having to deliver the bon mot, is revealed. Friends insisted to Greta Garbo that Levant's wit was legendary, that she had to meet him. When they were introduced, Levant fumbled, "I'm sorry, I didn't catch the name," to Garbo, perhaps the most famous woman in the world at the time. To her witty if not especially sensitive credit, Garbo rejoined, "Perhaps it's better if some legends remain legends."

The sobriquet of "the wit" is something of a literary consolation prize, a melancholy distinction for writers and performers whose other work doesn't overshadow what they managed to say. Even Oscar Wilde, perhaps the wit's wit, the name that seems a synonym, practically an eponym for wit, who did write, after all, *The Importance of Being Earnest*, *De Profundis*, "The Ballad of Reading Gaol," lives most vividly where his reputation was first made: in his creation of himself as the outré wit, the decadent, a sower of verbal anarchy in the balanced sentences of epigrams. And perhaps that's the magic of wit: it's combustible, anarchic, but perfectly composed and timed, as though it were a form whose internal tensions make it seem almost impossible, which may be why we value it. It's thought turned into writing in the context of the moment, with supernal cleverness. But ironically, most of our greatest wits haven't been our greatest writers: Johnson, Wilde, Parker, Sheridan. Of course, the melancholy idea asserts itself that wit is frequently a social form of communication. Clearly, Shakespeare was witty, as was Pope; we know that

Lamb was witty, of course, because he occasionally quotes himself, and says in his "autobiography" that he is "more apt to discharge his occasional conversations in a quaint aphorism or a poor quibble, than in set and edifying speeches, and has consequently been libeled as a person always aiming at wit, which as he told a dull fellow that charged him with it, is at least as good as aiming at dullness." Lamb, of course, was a melancholic of the first order, whose own bout with black bile had to take a back seat to his care for his sister, Mary, who had killed their mother when he was all of twenty-one.

But we need a recording audience, or a recording medium to capture the spirit of wit in its performance. I'm distinguishing the wit of conversation from literary wit. In the case of Wilde or Parker or Levant, the recording has to be a combination of self-preservation in the form of written reportage and self-reportage such as the reprinting in newspapers, in letters, repeated in memoirs. Or in Levant's recreations of his own witticisms on film. Wit is usually the most transitory of verbal arts. Do you remember the wittiest things you've said? And how many of them weren't spoken to an audience at all but murmured to yourself on the street, or caustically said under your breath at a lecture. The world is full of the ghosts of buried witticisms, the most anonymous of genres. Wit has an audience problem. But if your ego is large, like Wilde's, you capture your witticisms as epigrams. Parker and Levant were surrounded by writers, newspaper- men and women, columnists. What they said was written down, or passed around as liberally as the *Tatler* and the *Spectator*. After awhile they were expected to be witty. They were expected to say something memorable, and it was remembered.

Watching the few Oscar Levant clips that remain from the

late '50s, especially the kinescopes from his appearances on Paar, is fascinating and painful, partially because they seem so anachronistic—we don't associate painful self-revelation and self-laceration with the late '50s. With Lenny Bruce, perhaps, but not on national TV. Levant went on Jack Paar, and Paar, to his discredit, seemed to find Levant just clownishly amusing. "For every pearl that comes out of his mouth," Paar said, "a pill goes in." Levant said to Paar, "You know, when you're suffering from deep depression, you cannot make a decision. I first had deep apathy, then relapsed into deep depression. How I long for those deep apathy days." One thinks of Spalding Gray, years later, crafting monologues out of his life, entertaining, amusing, playing with the line between performance and persona—as Woody Allen had done in the early '60s—while, as we see Gray in his diaries, wondering whether the creation had gotten the better of him, whether he was locking himself into a performance he'd rather shake, he too, an obsessive hypochondriac. (The joke around Hollywood was that Levant's epitaph was going to be, "I told you I was sick.") In his diaries, Gray writes, "It is not enjoyable or easy for me to have a non-narrated private experience and I've always known that."

Levant's biographers write that "by the mid-thirties, Levant had turned his anxieties into topics of conversation—he had begun to invent the character of Levant the Neurotic, an invention based on his real neuroses. He was, in essence, playing himself, but the line between the real and the acted would always remain blurred." And he seemed to be able to manage the line to some extent until his heart attack in 1953, picking up an obsession here and a compulsion there: like the number of cigarettes that could be in an ashtray, or what couldn't be said to him before he performed. ("Good luck" brought him into a fury; in the *Barkleys of Broadway* [1949], before he performs Tchaikovsky's first piano concerto, if you're paying close attention, you can hear him saying "goodbye" to two stagehands before he goes on stage.)

Dorothy Kilgallen writes in a column in the late '30s that "he refers to himself always as a neurotic, but when someone asked him, 'Are you really neurotic or is it just a pose?' he looked up blandly and said, 'I guess it's just a pose.'" But like Robert Benchley, who became trapped by his role as the confused public speaker in films like *Road to Utopia* and *I Married a Witch*, or later Woody Allen's persona as the neurotic character as leading man (whose character, the film director, is assailed in *Stardust Memories* by fans of his "earlier, funnier" persona), the indelible character who borrows from his public persona is in danger of not being able to give the character back.

By the time of Jack Paar in the late '50s, Levant had metamorphosed from the public neurotic to the country's first public mental patient. He said to Paar, "If I have an argument with my wife, she has me committed. The ambulance is at our house quite frequently. It's a hell of a way to win an argument."

Through it all Levant's ability to produce memorable, even brilliant, lines remained undiminished. He was an extraordinary autodidact. Jean Peters, whom he dated for a while in the '30s, called him "the only brain in Hollywood." His talky memoirs are full of casual references to Rimbaud, Dostoevsky, Proust, Oscar Wilde. Levant says (in *Amnesiac*) of a performance at the Hollywood Bowl that it was "wrought out of my own originality, with the help of extra-sensory perception, somnolence at the moments when I wasn't playing, and out-and-out passages of Coleridge and De Quincey—when the world adumbrated the last vestige of the peripheral boundary of reality, and unreality." Not to mention his musical range—he could play anything from Beethoven to Copland, ragtime to Kern, and did play with Ormandy, Toscanini, Beecham. But connecting music and life, he said, "Instant unconsciousness has been my greatest passion.... My life is a morbid rondo.... Every moment is an earthquake to me."

I remember the poet Robert Creeley telling me about meeting Beckett in Paris. I'm just a one-eyed American poet who no one's ever heard of, he said to Beckett, in some grotto of a bar in Paris, but your work is so bleak, what keeps you writing? He said Beckett said he wrote in search of the perfect word, which was "small, and round and speckled." Perhaps wits are searching for the perfect line, straight and sharp and speckled, since wit is linear, but also frequently defensive—it draws attention and shoots down any response. Wit is usually a closed system, and self-referential. We call wit razor sharp, yes, but we also talk about mordant wit. They aren't binaries, the deathly and the razor. Think of anything Dorothy Parker said or wrote. "You might as well live," indeed. "Razors pain you," but they're also the sharp edge of aggression. Razor sharp wit frequently cuts both ways. "Anger was my chief raison d'être," Levant said in *Amnesiac*. "The first thing I do in the morning is brush my teeth and sharpen my tongue."

He said, mordantly, sharply, and with melancholy wit: "Judy Garland has become the living F. Scott Fitzgerald of Song" (*Amnesiac*, 187), and, "My behavior has been impeccable; I've been unconscious for six months," and, "Happiness isn't something you experience; it's something you remember." One wonders if part of the melancholy of wit is saying something admirable, if you're dubious about being something admirable.

In *De Profundis*, after his love object, Bosie, has lured him into fatal error and cast him off, Wilde is still crafting epigrams and aphorisms about his genius and the betrayal of his genius, and his incredible stupidity at hooking his bright star to a millstone. He's pinioned between accusation and self-accusation—I think that's one of the real fascinations of *De Profundis*, psychologically. Humility isn't a philosophy. It's an act of recognition. And Wilde is still bitterly angry in *De Profundis*, despite all attempts at achieving a stasis of reconciliation. He writes, "I made up my mind to live, but to wear gloom as a king wears purple: never to smile again: to turn whatever house I entered into a house of mourning: to make my friends walk slowly in sadness with me: to teach them that melancholy is the true secret of life: to maim them with an alien sorry: to mar them with my own pain." His own recognition is partial, though, as he continues, mournfully, to write, "Nobody is worthy to be loved. . . . Or if that phrase seems to you a bitter one to hear, let us say that everyone is worthy of love, except he who thinks that he is." Perhaps the supreme vice is making anyone feel that way. Poor Oscar. Oscars. "It is always twilight in one's cell, as it is always midnight in one's heart," Oscar Wilde writes in *De Profundis*, and that sounds like a kind of epitome of melancholy, a kind of rhapsody in blue.

CELESTE HOLM SYNDROME
THE EYES OF SISTER SCHOLASTICA

Kevork Djansezian (Hollywood couldn't work with that?) was born in Brooklyn in 1917 and died in Manhattan. She was the original Ado Annie of *Oklahoma* and a sharp, well-dressed character in *All about Eve*; *Gentleman's Agreement*; *The Tender Trap*; *High Society*; and many other films. She is stupidly ignored or thrown over by Gregory Peck, Jack Carson, Frank Sinatra, *and* Frank Sinatra (*sic*) in favor of supposedly more glamorous (ha!) and marginally younger women. But who could be more glamorous than Celeste Holm. I have Celeste Holm syndrome: a permanent chip on my shoulder about Hollywood's sexually undermining interesting "mature" women when their roles called for economic power or independence. In this I know I'm not alone, but the male gaze dominating as it does, these films manage to remain in the pantheon despite their abominable gender politics. Here I'm specifically thinking as well of the quartet of Eleanor Parker (*Sound of Music*), Eve Arden (almost everything), Nina Foch (*An American in Paris*)

6. Celeste Holm. Wikimedia Commons.

7. Nina Foch. Columbia Pictures / Wikimedia Commons.

8. Eve Arden. New York Public Library Digital Collections, Billy Rose Theatre Collection.

9. Eleanor Parker. Warner Bros. / Wikimedia Commons.

and, again, Celeste Holm in the aforementioned films. Because these women were interesting and powerful in their roles, vibrantly sexual, verbally playful, self-aware, and forward in their intentions, they end up humiliated, disposed, cast aside for ingenues: Julie Andrews is the choice of the Captain in *Sound of Music*; Leslie Caron gets spirited away at the end of *American in Paris*, leaving Nina Foch flat-footed; in *My Dream Is Yours*, Jack Carson melts away from his attachment to Eve Arden into the young Doris Day's lyrical enticements. And then there's Celeste Holm, a kind of avatar of urban chic, too together, I suppose, to go to the romantic school in which the men are the teachers, choose who's in the class, and shut the door, definitively, behind them.

Celeste Holm was thirty for *Gentleman's Agreement*, thirty-eight and thirty-nine for *The Tender Trap* and *High Society*, respectively.

Eleanor Parker was forty-three in *The Sound of Music*.

Eve Arden was forty-one in *My Dream Is Yours*.

Nina Foch was, astonishingly, twenty-seven when she filmed *An American in Paris*—aren't you surprised? (I was)—twelve years younger than Gene Kelly, the man she is the "older woman" to, the young man she's "setting up." She is certainly playing a woman in her late thirties or early forties, though: a *woman*, as opposed to the gamine girl-ness, the unformedness of Leslie Caron barely post-teenager.

That Hollywood wasn't and hasn't been hospitable to women is both a painful understatement and lacks nuance. Just saying that Hollywood was a site of degradation can't begin to speak to the achievements, against odds, of Bette Davis, Ida Lupino, or Katherine Hepburn. Nevertheless, it, Hollywood, meaning the major studios and production companies controlled by men from the second decade of and throughout the twentieth century and into the twenty-first, has been a model and molder of patriarchal treatment and representations of women. And I have always linked these four women, in my mind, to a very specific kind of degradation, the kind that speaks to the atrophied and damaging desires of men for younger women, pliant women, women who are teachable, educable, and whose power wasn't commensurate, or even threatening.

I want to speak to this group of women and their humiliations in these films, which have always pained me deeply, their situations a strange cathexis for me, what they offered seemingly too obvious, to me if not Gene Kelly, Sinatra, Christopher Plummer, and so on. The one twinge I have is Jack Carson, whose genial desperation and general confusion, whose character actor traits of self-defeat made him less despicable than the leading men who tossed these women over so stupidly. But first I want to speak to my central billing in this essay, Celeste Holm, and why, for me, she shines as a character actress.

Celeste Holm is not a character actress in quite the same way as Eve Arden, bringing a distinct persona from role to role (in Arden's case, the jaunty but caring amanuensis who can deliver a line with asperity, frequently at her own expense). She does bring a kind of fractured persona to *some* of her roles, not dissimilar from Eve Arden's qualities: urban, independent, wisecracking. But Holm also disappears into different kinds of roles on occasion, as in her Oscar-nominated role as Sister Scholastica in *Come to the Stable*, where she plays a theological sidekick (the sidekick a character actor specialty) to Loretta Young.

I love watching Holm as Sister Scholastica (almost as much as I like saying "Sister Scholastica"—how about that for the next Marvel hero) just to get lost in the movement of her eyes. The film itself is a rather disposable piece of sentimental post-war kitsch about nuns wanting to build a hospital for injured children in Connecticut. They've come from France with a mission and need to get the deed from a mobster whose son died in action: holy creaking plot lines, Batman! And here I must admit a terminal objection to Loretta Young. Forever not Loretta Young for me. I find her straightforward sincerity medicinal. And I don't watch movies to be cured of anything, other than melancholy and cinema-deprivation. Loretta Young is not the medicine for my melancholy—she makes me want to go to an anarchist convention. I can't stand that much concentrated self-satisfaction.

And here, in homage to the eyes of Celeste Holm, I must digress to (do we digress to, or from—is a digression losing a trail, or finding one?), a story, told by Stephen Sondheim, paraphrased: Ethel Merman was on the Loretta Young TV show in the late 1950s and kept cursing during rehearsals, as was her wont. Young, strict with conventional morality, had a curse jar, to keep all in line as good mouth-washed children. How she managed this in Hollywood is a mystery. But Merman slipped, and Young said, Miss Merman, please put fifty cents in the jar. Merman later said, "Shit, I forgot my line." Young: "Please, Miss Merman, my rules." Another payment to the jar. A third infraction, Merman saying, "Damn it, missed my spot." She could see Young walking toward her and cut her off, saying, "Here's five bucks, Loretta, and go fuck yourself." I love that story, as does Sondheim, apparently—he tells it frequently.

Come to the Stable was written by Claire Boothe Luce—such a complex American woman—in her transitional period. She had written *The Women*, one of the early feminist works of American theater, campaigned for suffrage, campaigned for Roosevelt. After her daughter was killed in a car accident in 1944, she converted to Roman Catholicism and became increasingly conservative. She wrote *Come to the Stable* in 1946, filmed in 1949. The purity of the nuns, and the relative humorlessness of the script, the atmosphere of postwar exhaustion, and the forced miracles and epiphanies are unconvincing, to say the least. Loretta Young is like a bulldozer, all certainty and stolidity.

But Celeste Holm, by her side, younger, somewhat bewildered, looks at everything as though it had just come to life, as though attention were the quality that the weary world needed most. It is a quality she brings to all her roles—despite being known for how well she snaps a line. Henry Koster, the mid-list director of *Come to the Stable*, keeps her in the background. But had the film been shot by Roberto Rossellini, he would have shot her face in half white, half shadowed light, to bring out her extraordinarily asymmetric beauty. I've always been attracted to women who were sometimes beautiful, sometimes not. I remember being enthralled, in my teens, seeing Jeanne Moreau for the first time, how scene to scene, in *Jules et Jim*, she could look ravishing or plain. I think something of this early fascination has followed in tastes in non-cinematic women (note how my life outside of film is modified by film). Women whose looks varied, whose beauty had character that made their appearance changeable were always more interesting to me than the pleasantries of fixed symmetries.

Celeste Holm's face: it captures me. I have Celeste Holm

syndrome. I can't think straight when I look at her. She's too interesting, too sympathetic, but not too sympathetic. If that makes sense. Her eyes are large, pale blue, we see in the color films, but more perceptive than anything, and they seem to exist in an impossible distance from her long, elegant neck. Her nose is aquiline with a slight turn down, giving an impression of a slightly pretty birdliness in some images, especially from an angle. Photographed straight on she can radiate a sudden wild symmetry, but smiling, she becomes a bit toothy, with a large smile. Her smile twists, her mouth is expressive, so we follow the nuances of her voice, her instrument, as she uses it, plays it, to return to the eyes for the register of what she herself has just said.

In *Tender Trap* we first see Celeste Holm playing the violin in an orchestra, and her voice is a bit like a string instrument. It has range, great melody, but can also crack and perform dissonances when it has to. It should be named for her: *violoncele*. Celeste Holm has one of the most playful voices of Hollywood actresses, and her vocal range establishes the range of persona, part of what stretches our sense of character, in film and with each other. Think of the distinct voices you know, the way their warmth or quirkiness, or their icy trebling of self brings them to sudden distillation—a sudden frisson of memories accompanies the sounds of the voice. We think of the legendary quality of cinema's classic visages: Bogart's asymmetry, his rough beauty; Joan Crawford's full lips and dark eyes, the way she flashes a kind of unknowable depth and wildness in her face. But voice is just as important—Barbara Stanwyck's quirky disguise of her Brooklyn accent into something like East Coast with aspirations; the Bogart lisp; the earnestness inherent in Gregory Peck's deep bass; Robert

Ryan's snaky breathiness, voice cracking (has any actor used breath better?). For character actors, much of the character is in voice: Edward Everett Horton's comic strip upper-class New York (though he, too, was born in Brooklyn); Thelma Ritter's working-class Brooklyn accent, always seemingly on the verge of impatience in its edginess (I seem to be stuck on New York here); or Eric Blore, whose English accent is almost always surreally inflated, extended, so that vowels become epic things, cartoon arias.

I think I'm especially sensitive to the lingering effects of voice because I've been haunted for so many years by the slowly disappearing memory of my mother's voice. My mother died almost forty years ago, in my very early twenties. This was way before the digital age, and no tape recordings or films with sound exist with her voice inscribed. The inscription of her voice in my memory is a tenuous affair—at times I think I remember it, at other times it's an aural flicker, something heard in a dream, or from two rooms away, almost heard. She, incidentally, had a Brooklyn accent, which was always a curiosity since she was born in rural New Jersey, only moving to the Midwood section of Brooklyn in her teens. Go figure.

But it is perhaps because of her that I listen so closely to voices, and that I take such special pleasure in the voices whose registers *register* with me. Such is the case with Celeste Holm's voice. Listen to her revive her show-stopping number from the original production of *Oklahoma*; she was the original Ado Annie, and her "I Can't Say No" is definitive, full of sly restraint, perfect for a song about the limits of restraint. She sings it years later on Ed Sullivan—you can see the kinescope on YouTube—but it seems like little has been lost in the twelve years between her original performance in 1943 and the TV version of '55. Holm's voice, unlike Gloria Grahame's exaggerated sexpot version in the film, is full of half-knowing reservations, uncertainty that taboo and desire are reconcilable, until, her eyes coming alive, she seems to convince herself that they are, and the generic hayseed accent she sings with, softened by her native and suppressed sophistication, gets warmer and more confident: she can't say no, but that's okay with her and just fine with us—she sings half a lament and half a seduction of us.

Listen to Holm say to David Wayne in *The Tender Trap*, "The night is young, we're middle-aged. Anything could happen." Yes, the writing is tart, but Holm delivers it with a blend of gentle, self-aware self-mockery that is anything but bathetic; it's actually a calibration of absurdity and possibility, fluted through her mezzo delivery with something like upbeat rue. That's a complex instrument, the voice just breaking like a small wave.

In *All about Eve*, one of Holm's most well-known roles, as Karen Richards, best friend to Bette Davis's Margo Channing, Holm serves as a kind of agent provocateur, setting the plot in motion ("Nothing you've ever done has made me as happy as taking Eve in," she tells Margo, after Karen introduces the serpent into the garden of their friendship, in a misguided attempt to "correct" Margo's inflated ego and give the ingenue actor, Eve, a break, as Margo's understudy). And it is Celeste Holm who serves the volley, delivered in perfect friction between understanding and exhaustion—the continuum of a friendship pushed to its limits—asking Bette Davis's Margo, "Is it over or just beginning," in response to her building frustration and fury. Davis's response is, of course, one of the great delivered lines of cinema: "Fasten your seatbelts. It's going to be a bumpy night." It's easy to forget in the white-hot greatness of the Davis riposte, how good the setup is, and why Holm is so right as the tolerant foil for her—her voice the tonic to Davis's gin, her face the unembittered Modigliani contrast to Bette Davis's weathered cusp of beauty.

The Celeste Holm performance that most captivates me and infuriates me is her Ann Dettrey in Elia Kazan's *Gentleman's Agreement* (1947), written by Moss Hart, based on Laura Z. Hobson's postwar novel about antisemitism. Holm plays the fashion editor at the magazine where Gregory Peck, as Phil Green, is masquerading as a Jew to write his expose. And here I have to say that while few actresses seem as permanently stylish as Holm (her clothes always tailored perfectly—she defines the *handsome* woman, and I mean that as a high compliment) no one ever looked better in a hat. Perhaps it was because of the slight asymmetry of her face, her tendency to wear them at a slightly jaunty angle, but hats and Holmes were made for each other. "Does anyone still wear a hat?" Elaine Stritch famously sang in the original incarnation of Stephen Sondheim's *Company*. Celeste Holm is hatted for eternity. "We're sophisticated New Yorkers," she tells Phil Green (Peck) near the beginning of *Gentleman's Agreement*, and she looks it.

But it's a muted sophistication that Holm brings across, a wry sophistication, at times self-mocking. She's been around, taken the measure of things, of herself. She's proportionate and has a sense of proportion. Perhaps it's this quality of self, of strength, among the women I mention earlier that makes them such targets for the rejecting scenario of cinematic narratives. Because these women project assurance, age plus wisdom plus sexual power, they have to be crippled by a film's assertion that they aren't *preferred* by their male protagonists, by Frank Sinatra, Gene Kelly, Christopher Plummer, or Gregory Peck. These mid-century male stars need ingenues, ingenuousness embodied in youth, not the company of ripe companionship.

Nina Foch, Celeste Holm, Eleanor Parker, Eve Arden: here I have to digress to talk briefly about why each, sharing some of the qualities of Celeste Holm, is ill-treated by the dull-witted men and masculinist frames of their films, and how this has ruined each of the lauded films in question, for me.

In *American in Paris* Gene Kelly (Jerry Mulligan) plays, of all things, an aspiring painter. It just doesn't work. He's too jumpy, too insouciant in his remarks about art. Thank goodness for Oscar Levant, constantly rendering the film watchable by undercutting the postwar peppy American self-congratulatory mayhem with sardonic asides. But Kelly wants to paint (his paintings in the film are exceptionally ordinary Postimpressionist images) and he does have one advocate: Milo Roberts, played by Nina Foch, an "older" woman who takes an interest in Kelly (she was twelve years younger), clearly enamored of him. Surreal age disparities are nothing novel in Hollywood films. (Although more often than not, a man is courting a woman young enough to be his daughter or his granddaughter. Lillian Gish was quoted as saying, "You know, when I first went into the movies Lionel Barrymore played my grandfather. Later he played my father and finally he played my husband. If he had lived I'm sure I would have played his mother. That's the way it is in Hollywood. The men get younger and the women get older.") Jessie Royce Landis played Cary Grant's mother in *North by Northwest* despite being eight years older than him. James Stewart at fifty-four played a young recent law school graduate courting the thirty-three-year-old Vera Miles in *The*

Man Who Shot Liberty Valance. The list is endless. But Nina
Fochs's "older" heiress who "sets up" Gene Kelly, giving him
a room of his own to paint in, enabling his career, and clearly
loving him, implicitly (it's 1951 and MGM) sleeping with him
in premonitory shades of, a decade later, Patricia Neal (who
might be included in our pantheon, as well) and George
Peppard's arrangement. It is clearly a strange age inversion.
Because she pursues Kelly, in other words displays sexual
agency, it seems, in the emotional logic of the film, she must
be betrayed and rejected. She's beautiful, realistic, supportive.
Oh, and wealthy: another form of agency—economic. In the
cultural milieu of 1951, these aren't recommendations. The
gamine Leslie Caron, reasonably unformed, girlish, depen-
dent, is the natural choice for Kelly once Foch enables him
to create a facsimile of an ego. If it weren't for Vincente
Minnelli's wildly bold choreography of costume and color
in scene, and a few of the dances (and Oscar, Oscar Levant!)
I could hardly bear to watch "The Sacrificial Desecration
of Nina Foch" (otherwise known as *An American in Paris*).
She's used, ditched. What is presented as the romantic end
of the long impressionist ballet, culminating in the getaway
(forget the marriage of convenience between Leslie Caron and
Georges Guetary, the man who saved her during the war) is
a poem of ingratitude—leave those who save you, those who
nurture you, for the abstract dance of love. If they happen to
be women who are, by all appearances to us, the cinematic
audience, remarkable, beautiful and, well, "mature," well, all is
fair in love after war. Just ask Milo Roberts. Look, I know I've
written about this in an earlier essay. Perhaps you can chalk
it up as one of the less-reported symptoms of Celeste Holm
syndrome, a tendency to sympathize with around-midcentury

actresses, who seem brutalized by the excesses of Hollywood's cult of the Galatea-like young woman.

I assume not everyone is as bothered as I am that the Baron von Trapp (Christopher Plummer) leaves his magnificently wealthy Austrian socialite fiancée, Baroness Elsa von Schraeder (Eleanor Parker), for his children's young nanny, played by the irresistible Julie Andrews. Parker was forty-three when the film was made, and ravishing. Her hair, like two blonde vortices on either side of her head, expectant and vulnerable blue eyes, and dressed throughout to show off her slimness, in clothes that are tailored, meaning tight, in lamé and twill fabrics whose frictions all but call out their cost, their essence of taste. The highbrow Eleanor Parker's baroness projects a raw sexual desire for the baron, the baroness wanting her baron. The sexual tension between Plummer and Parker is strong, the kind that eviscerates anyone else around: children, nannies. But Plummer also has sexual chemistry with Julie Andrews, Fraulein Maria, and she is poor, and young, and virginal. Her desires are subservient to her role as mother in training.

I've always loved Parker in *The Sound of Music* because she defines a kind of midcentury decadent elegance, and her presentation of the baroness seems, for the most part, a study in honest decadence, which appeals to me. She knows herself, which always appeals to me, even if I sometimes succumb to a slight queasiness at her voraciousness. Robert Wise presents her, through much of the film, as a foil, a friction in our sense of female possibilities—lopsided distaff powers. This is no virgin/whore binary; it's a virgin/sexually hungry middle-aged woman binary, with the film tilting toward the virgin. But the virgin has to win the contest, uneasy as Ernest Lehman, the great screenwriter, or more likely Howard Lindsay and Russel

Crouse who wrote the original book (they *did* write *Life with Father*), is about the matchup, by a playing field that's titled, stilted. Julie Andrews has abundant charms, but we are meant to be swayed against Eleanor Parker because she doesn't like children, demonstrated by her playing ball with them in high heels, like a dimwit, and in a creaky expositional plot move, she tells the baron's friend Max Detweiler (Richard Haydn) that she's going to ship the children off to boarding school. It's bad mother syndrome, in *antecessum*.

But I always feel that Eleanor Parker's love is a mature, hot-burning love. Like Nina Foch in *American in Paris*, she's got money, desire she knows how to express, and a dead husband. But the men see through these ghosted women to the young virgins waiting beyond them. I don't like it. It feels violent and punishing. Eleanor Parker, who is reprieved in her sendoff, apparently chastened by rejection, looks to me in the end like a sacrifice to the Virgin Maria. But even as she's thrown over, bathed in Robert Wise's purifying soft and gauzy light, tarred with the attempted distraction of our gaze by the moral damnation attached to her wealthy step-parental scheming, I can't help responding to the virtue of her intensity, since, after all, she loves deeply, unabashedly, and no one ever wore a skintight dress while addressing love's impossibility from the desperation in her eyes with a more alluring combination.

And here I return to the sine qua non of the brilliantly jilted, and the subject of my essay: Celeste Holm, Holm as Ann Dettrey in *Gentleman's Agreement*.

For those of you who don't remember Kazan's film, Holm, as stylish as ever, playing a New York fashion editor, decidedly single, is singular as a non-prejudiced attendant to Gregory Peck's Phil Green masquerade as Jew to expose anti-Semitism for the magazine they both work for. Peck is smitten with Dorothy McGuire's Kathy Lacy, who scene after scene demonstrates her clueless Westchester *well-intentioned* class bias, anti-Semitism, and general dopiness. While McGuire is having to say things like "heck, I didn't know asking someone not to mention they were Jewish was anti-Semitic" (a paraphrase) the sharp-witted and sharply dressed Holm, spending time with Peck's Jewish buddy (he's not named Buddy in the film, he's named Dave(!), played with downbeat intensity by John Garfield) is cracking lines like, "Every man who seems attractive is either married or barred on a technicality," or, "Mirror, mirror on the wall, who's the most brilliant of them all. That mirror ain't no gentleman." Celeste Holm's delivery is Eve Ardenish: sharp and rueful, but a bit softer. Just as songwriters loved writing for Fred Astaire because he could syncopate their melodies and articulate their lyrics so well, screenwriters (Ben Hecht, Moss Hart, Herman Mankiewicz) loved writing lines for Celeste Holm because her delivery was so precise that their sentences were—well—syncopated by her.

Watching this film there is a subtle sense of inevitability, unlike in *American in Paris*, where Minnelli and Kelly and Alan Jay Lerner have the strength of their bad conviction throughout the film that of course Kelly is going to dump the lovely Nina Foch for Leslie Caron. The opposite *seems* true when you watch Kazan's *Gentleman's Agreement*. You think, of course Gregory Peck is going to leave Dorothy McGuire for Celeste Holm. For one thing, she's Celeste Holm. For another, she's not anti-Semitic and supports his project. For another, she's wearing those great hats and she's the fashion editor (I know I said that already). What's more, she's completely hit it off with best friend Dave (here, we veer off into wish fulfillment). Holm's delicate look of empathetic despair when Garfield is called a *Yid* in a nightclub is heartbreaking. So how could anyone pass on the chance of spending his days with John Garfield and Celeste Holm, you ask? The calculus of that is impossible to refute, to refuse: the stylish, supportive wife, the sharp, Jewish war-buddy who thinks (wisely—that Dave!) she's perfecto.

You know the answer to that question. Holm's fashionable supportiveness, her fastidious self-awareness in character—"Everybody loves Ann," she says sardonically, the cracked ice of rejection in the general acclaim accompanied by a muted half-laugh—is doomed to metarejection, the woman whose character is perennially single must stay single to support the prevailing gender tropes of what becomes of an independent and free-thinking single woman in her thirties. "One little action on one little front," she says, makes all the difference, driving home the Kazanian social message (if not Kazan's lived action). Hurray for that, but when Gregory Peck's Green, responding to her direct attention near the end of *Gentleman's Agreement*, asks, "Are you proposing, Ann?" it's the seal of her social doom. She's too forthcoming, too straight in not letting any bigoted tripe get past her, too overt in her intentions. In short, she's fully formed, not teachable, which is the death spiral for all the women, all the characters I've been discussing. Who gets the embrace, the nod, the eternal return? Kathy Lacy (Dorothy McGuire), of course (the name itself makes me a little sick, dripping as it is of gender-y associations, that double "y," my double "*why?*").

Where does this leave us? And what happened to Celeste Holm after her character turns in some of the most canonical films of the '50s? She did some theater and lots of forgettable

TV, though I remember, even as a child, my parents lighting up when she appeared: look, it's Celeste Holm!—as though something special had happened, or was about to. This aura is the comet's tail of the character actor and perhaps the actor past her prime—prime measured in the terms of highest visibility, or greatest commercial success, not artistic power. Like writers, actors should age well, or interestingly, but it doesn't always seem possible, especially for women, which is to say we don't let them or see them.

Nevertheless, Ms. Holm lived on at her Central Park apartment, purchased for ten thousand dollars in 1953 with her earnings from *All about Eve*. At her death in 2012, at the age of ninety-five, it was worth an estimated ten million. Holm had been living there with her third husband, an opera singer. He was forty-one.

DOUBLE TAKE

JACK CARSON *AGONISTES*

I've always loved a good double take, the head seeming to almost involuntarily whip again toward the direction it was just pointing, the direction the eyes were just looking, as though it needed, *they* needed, to really register what had just been seen or heard, to take in what had been passed over. Usually, what hadn't been registered was something slightly shocking, but muted, a strange juxtaposition unexpected in its context: a woman half-dressed in a store window—not a mannequin; a goat in the back seat of a cab; an insult dressed as a compliment: "I'm sure no one would ever make the mistake of overestimating your intelligence." "The senses cannot decide . . . being themselves full of uncertainty," Montaigne writes in "Apology for Raymond Sebond." "To judge the appearances of things, we need a judicatory instrument," he writes, a secondary response, which he posits as reason. Maybe it's the little click of reason that causes the double take, like an inner Rube Goldberg mechanism: our protagonist half smiles

10. Jack Carson. New York Public Library Digital Collections, Billy Rose Theatre Collection.

as if the world is in its natural order, as if nothing is amiss, then wrenches his head in the direction of the deception, the distortion, the uncanny image, usually with a grimace or a look of stark perplexity.

What I love about these second looks, these doubled takes on what has just happened—which if you pay attention you're apt to really catch from time to time—is that they capture the distilled sense that the world isn't what it seems. Kant writes that "all appearances are real and *negatio*; sophistical: all reality must be sensation." "Real and *negatio*" (denied or refused): so when we become aware of the anomaly, we look again, we *double* look.

Actors who rely frequently on the double take—Jack Carson, Groucho Marx, Oliver Hardy, Edward Everett Horton, Lucille Ball, Marty Feldman, and so on—stand in for our sense of the world's cracks and fissures, its uncanniness. The uncanniness, to go back to Freud's sense of *heimlich* and *unheimlich*, at home or disoriented, is frequently, in language, the actor's (standing in for our own) sense of being at home or alienated in language itself; language being the world we live in that is full of appearance and sophistry, text and subtext. Yes, the brilliance of the double take is that it can summarize the uncanny in a second-long gesture. What had at first seemed familiar or safe, is not. The unexpected, the wildly coincidental, the *unheimlich* jolts us: we move from order to disorder, looking again where we just looked, where everything seemed, just moments ago, reasonable. The double take is frequently a subcategory of the surreal: think of Groucho telling Chico he wants to add a "sanity clause" to the contract, turning again to Chico after he hears him say, "There's no such thing as Sanity Clause."

The term "double take" is indelibly cinematic and dates

from silent film, where actors from Charlie Chaplin to Ben Turpin to James Finlayson to Harry Langdon did a second look, or "take" in movie terms. A related though less well-known term is the "spit take," where an actor takes a drink that seems normal and realizes he has gotten something awful in his mouth and spits it out. The comic premise, in any case, is that things aren't what they seem, sound, taste, and walking by, paying scant attention, not really looking and hearing, we miss the strange, and interesting even if unsettling paradoxes and performances, tableaux and testimonies the world is constantly gracing and threatening us with.

It's in this way that I think of Jack Carson, who was a great master of the double take, a kind of working-class representative of Bergson in cinema, reminding us to look again, to really listen. Bergson warns us against the dulled out senses of living in the modern world—we aren't really seeing and hearing; that's the first look. The second look or take is the revival, the coming to life of the senses really registering that goat, that woman. "Sanity Claus?"—what? Jack Carson was known as "king of the double take."

Agonistes comes from the ancient Greek ἀγωνιστής, a contestant in the public games, and from ἀγών or *agôn*, a contest or struggle. In Milton's *Samson Agonistes*, Samson has an overt, an external, struggle against the Philistines, but more interestingly to Milton, an inner struggle, his blindness combined with power, his betrayal by his wife Dalila, his overarching feelings of vengeance.

My man here (not Godfrey), Jack Carson, also shows inner struggles, splits, in most of the characters he plays, though more often than not they're rendered comically. He, like

Samson, is bigger than most men—six feet two and hefty—and often his trouble, his actions, his divisions revolve around women. Frequently, he's both reasonably nice, wisecracking, worldly wise as the allegory says, but also, as character acting roles demand and the comic second lead requires: an absurd character, ridiculous in his white lying, opportunism, self-promotion. Nevertheless, we like him, at least I do. Why? Perhaps because of his struggle; his division; his constant double takes, attempts at corrective vision: to see better is to be better. To be clear, even for an instant (*did you ever go clear*) is to have a plenitude of possibilities, since we're refusing to be deceived by our bland acceptance of false appearances, and it perhaps even opens the possibility of change, though this is always an optimistic idea. In other words, certain kinds of division are dynamic, are interesting, even if (especially when?) some of the parts are absurd, unadmirable, even disreputable, *shady*. The better self hears what the weaker self would rather not, sees what one wishes one wouldn't. The double take can be a symbol of the struggle, as the parts of a character try to reconcile inner and outer worlds—he can't quite trust what he sees and hears because he can't completely trust himself: he has to look again; what did I hear? What did I see? His own divisions are externalized.

The *agon*, the public games, are the movies, and the struggle you could say is acting, or that it is present in Jack Carson's acting—even in his roles in light or romantic comedy.

Terms related to *agon* are "antagonist" and "protagonist," and these are relevant since Jack Carson wore the mantle of protagonist with difficulty, most often with comical anxiety.

Carson worked in films from 1910 to 1963. He was born in Canada, but he moved to Milwaukee as a boy, and this hometown identification stayed with him (see *Two Guys from Milwaukee* with his best friend, Dennis Morgan—his better-looking buddy in several films, also from Milwaukee) and became part of his unpretentious appeal. His characters, whether genial or slightly dyspeptic, tended to be working class, and part of Carson's arsenal of quizzical looks centered on a class-based sense that others were speaking a language he wasn't privy to, that he was missing out. This, I think, makes him sympathetic even when he (which is to say the character of his character) was not completely appealing, if that makes sense.

Despite his appearance in any number of B movies, Carson also appeared in four Oscar-nominated films: *Stage Door*, *Mr. Smith Goes to Washington*, *Mildred Pierce*, and *Cat on a Hot Tin Roof*, but he was also in many other "prestige" films such as *Bringing Up Baby*, *Arsenic and Old Lace*, *Blues in the Night*, and *Bright Leaf*. His voice was distinctive, slightly nasal, midwestern blue collar—he sounds like the apotheosis of "guy in a bar." Because of this easy identification, he did lots of radio work: plays, variety, announcing, and he had a brief TV variety show in the mid-'50s. But importantly, Carson got his start in vaudeville, on the infamous Orpheum circuit, doing a double act with a friend (he was always a perfect foil) with lots of slapstick and one-liners, his training ground. At six feet two inches tall and between 220 and 240 pounds, he knew how to take a fall, making it look painful and somewhat graceful at the same time, in the way of Oliver Hardy. (Perhaps we forget about the apprenticeships of character actors, thinking they wander on to the set with perfect timing and crafted personae.) By the time of Carson's first appearance (*Bringing Up Baby* [1938]) he had been acting in college, vaudeville, and radio for almost twenty years.

In general, Jack Carson carries with him a kind of cocky wince. He walks into a room as though he's looking to be congratulated and killed simultaneously—as though a surprise party were waiting to recognize his wonderfulness or a dead reckoning to call him on his perfidy. How can it, he, be both? He carries an expression that curdles as it emerges, that involuntarily turns on itself, and that's a large part of his attraction as a performer; despite his vanity, his vainglory, his duplicity in a given role, he generally looks as though he's about to pay for it in a moment's notice, which, I suppose, is a way of saying that his mien is frequently trying to conceal the guilty self-knowledge that he's a heel. This is a partial saving grace: that he telegraphs his original sin. And it creates a comedy of self, an internal battle externalized.

Carson's best-known role is probably Wally Fay in Michael Curtiz's *Mildred Pierce*. Carson worked with Curtiz several times in the '40s, in *Roughly Speaking, Mildred Pierce* (both 1945), *Romance on the High Seas* (1948), and *My Dream Is Yours* (1949). The latter two films co-star Doris Day in two of her earliest roles, and Carson is the leading man, so it's safe to say that Curtiz thought highly of him. It's easy to see why after watching *Mildred Pierce*.

In *Mildred Pierce* Carson plays Wally Fay, a business partner of Mildred's (Joan Crawford's) husband, and Mildred's partner to be; he ends up buying them both out in pragmatic and self-preserving business deals when the Pierce's fail. These are not quite unethical, merely opportunistic, which is how Carson presents Fay through much of the film. But Carson is arguably the most complex and unstable character in the film and, I would argue, is a large part of what makes Mildred Pierce more interesting than an overheated film noir, despite Joan Crawford's calibrated performance, Eve Arden's small but as predictably brilliant sardonic line deliveries, and Zachary Scott's memorable turn as a sleazy bankrupt roué. I've always found Ann Blyth's turn as Mildred's daughter from hell predictable and repetitive.

Carson, on the other hand, is not predictable. He's so full of unclaimed thoughts registered from scene to scene and contradictions in his Fay's relationship to Mildred that it's hard to know which side of his character will play from scene to scene. In *Mildred Pierce*, Carson has plenty of comic business, his forte, though mostly in the form of sarcastic line deliveries. He's a man on the make: from the beginning he's openly making sexual moves on Mildred with a kind of cavalier confidence that seems brazenly misplaced. Joan Crawford bats him away and Carson, the supposedly confident ladies' man, seems both undeterred (as in wait until next time) and slightly wounded (as in what's wrong with me). He can't quite understand why she's not interested, that she wouldn't be interested simply because she's not. That's his dull side, the side that can't seem to see past his ego, his self-interest. But this narrowness makes him vulnerable (this is true of many of the characters Carson plays, though many are less worldly than Wally Fay) and balances out the power between Mildred and him, his economic advantage. Carson has business savvy, Joan Crawford has sexual allure and wild aspirations, and between them a kind of *pas de deux* emerges, one or the other seeming to be leading—this hardly a new gender dynamic. But one of the central ironies about *Mildred Pierce* is that the fatal flaw of each character (with the exception of Vida, Mildred's daughter, played by Ann Blyth—*Vida*, life as unredeemable) reveals one of their best qualities, a light at the end of the hamartia.

Joan Crawford's Mildred is a guilty mother who gives much too much to her daughter because she feels responsible for the death of her younger daughter: her flaw is based on her maternal love and responsibility. Zachary Scott's Beragon, the bankrupt society heel, can't allow his actual feelings for Mildred to violate the purity of his parasitic use of her as a bankroll, and it is these actual feelings, revealed to Mildred's daughter backhandedly when he tells her that he won't marry her, and to only us when he murmurs Mildred's name as he falls to the floor after Vida shoots him, that ultimately lead to his death.

Carson cares for Mildred, too, and he is, in fact, the character who, other than Mildred, embodies the most complicated divisions in the film. He is ironically named Fay, since Carson is at first rather conventionally manly in *Mildred Pierce*, a straight guy on the make. If you don't know Carson well: large, broad shoulders, big head—there are jokes about his forehead in a couple of films. And as he aged he put on weight, so the sense of a man who is just, well, big (though not fat), something closer to paunchy, comes to mind. It's no wonder he was typecast as second lead or did so much comedy. But his vaudevillian physical dexterity—pratfalls, turnarounds, he has mobility—works against the size that in another man might seem stolid or clumsy. Here, in 1945, when Carson was just thirty-five, he still seems well built, solid.

When we first see him, he's under a sign for cocktails in a bar he owns, and Mildred has just been talked out of suicide on a bridge by a cop. He seems actually solicitous after noticing she's in trouble and then, as a fundamental opportunist, he comes on to her. Mildred—and this is the fascinating part of Joan Crawford's performance—is ultimately indomitable (which softens Carson's moves on her—she can handle anything), and she invites Wally to her place where she tries to set him up for the murder of her feckless second husband, Beragon. So right from the beginning of the film we get a complicated sense of who may or may not be in control, who is vulnerable, and we wonder about the sources and nature of betrayal, the depths and nature of character that led to such calumny, a classic film noir flashback structure.

"You can talk your way out of anything," Mildred says to Wally, and he does talk his way out of the murder rap she's tried to frame him with—but that isn't difficult. More difficult is talking his way *into* Mildred's sexual and romantic affections. One characteristic of Carson's character, here, and elsewhere, is that he talks and talks, frequently trying to convince someone of something dubious. From role to role it's one of the most identifiable of his characteristics: he's a man of words—strung together, his characters seem to have an inexhaustible faith in his ability to sell his own sincerity, even when it seems stale or overripe. When his arguments are punctured, when his logic is skewered, when he's rebuffed, he usually pouts a bit, frequently acknowledges the justness of his exposure, and moves on to his next argument, sometimes more pragmatically sincere, as though flippancy and low-grade guile didn't work so he might as well try to be honest. He's a very American character, a used car salesman of the self, wrapped around a kind of innocent: he knows he's deceitful, but he means no harm, a version of the flimflam man. The fact that he's so transparent is what makes him likeable, possible to be liked. People, women especially, are always looking at him cross-eyed, as the saying goes, because he's such an easy call. In a contemporary character/actor this might be seen as a second layer of deception, a trap used to bring defenses down, but Carson, a creature, a character of the '40s and '50s, is manifestly untrustworthy, not a manipulator. And half the time, or more in the comedies, he ends up the victim of his own misplayed machinations.

Such is the case in *Phffft*, a 1954 comedy directed by Mark Robson, starring Judy Holliday and Jack Lemon as a married couple who errantly divorce. Jack Carson plays the friend of the husband/new bachelor, Jack Lemon, who is going to liberate him into the pleasures of his singleness, show him the ropes and pleasures of bachelorhood, including a night with the ever-available Kim Novak (talk about unrestrained male fantasy; only in the movies would Kim Novak be good naturedly waiting around for an over-sexed, ridiculous lotharios and his protégé). A familiar and stereotypical role for Carson to step into, but as he preaches the role of sexual liberation (Holliday, too, is attempting her version of let's see what's out there and how this goes) Carson manages to make it interesting by performing his usual *agon*. Which is to say the life that he's trying to sell to Jack Lemmon never seems convincingly appealing: we think this car must have something wrong with it. In other words, Carson oversells, he's a tad desperate in pushing Jack Lemon toward *la dolce vita*. A lovely way of living, after all, sells itself; it doesn't really need desperate apostles with sweat on their upper lips and secret plans of when to dim the lights.

Carson comically reminds us that when we see and hear divisions, even when they make us laugh, they're usually because one part of the self isn't self-convinced. It's funny to watch a kind of double discourse in motion, and we're also reminded, lest we push him too far away as a model of perfect contradiction, that we too are contradictory. "Do I contradict myself? Very well then, I contradict myself," Montaigne writes in "On Repentance," capturing the wavering self. And unlike the stolid leading actors of so many films, unlike the heroic models of consistency of so many protagonists, Jack Carson, that pragmatic self-server, serves up the self as contradictory: the self as double, in his motives, never quite convinced, and therefore all the more convincing, and never completely whole, and therefore wholly believable.

Here, after this discussion of divisions in the self, I must stop and tell you something that I find disarming and completely charming. In the 1940s, Carson would disappear for weeks at a time. No one knew where he went, other than his then wife, Kay St. Germain Wells (whose name I may elope with in my dreams tonight—it has pretty possibilities for character development). There was speculation, of course: benders, a woman somewhere—the other side of this life. Actually, and completely improbably, Carson would escape back to the Midwest and perform for weeks at a time with the Clyde Beatty circus. He put on his makeup and performed anonymously, for scale, as a clown. Apparently the jig was up at some point when word seeped out and the thing could no longer be done in the only way he desired it: completely undercover. The only recorded comment of Carson's about this time is: "They loved me and my routines." Actors escape into characters, and character actors apparently need escape from their characters, as well; in Carson's case into an archetype of another kind of character. The frequently clownish character actor would become one of the clowns. The self is mysterious, as any essayist or actor can avow—and personae are sticky and seductive. How must it have felt to become a character that is completely devoted to the essence of *fool*, those strange creatures that developed from the *commedia dell'arte* and the harlequinade? The modern circus clown, inspired by Joseph Grimaldi in the early 1800s, was based on Tom Belling's Auguste, or red clown, in the later decades of the nineteenth century. Here, a player could act wide swaths of emotions, torrents of sudden happiness or sadness—maybe that was part it, how large and uncomplicated the emotional register as opposed to the more calibrated performances of film. But the clown itself, for many of us, is itself an uncanny figure, a figure begging for our own take, to make sure we've read him right, caught the register. Then again, as a character actor who had made it, was in constant demand, perhaps the answer is as simple as: escape from Hollywood and fame.

To return to *Mildred Pierce*: part of the reason Jack Carson's performance in *MP* remains his most well known, or perhaps is considered his most quintessential, is that it distills most distinctly the element of self-loathing that is latent in the mix of wiseacre and know-it-all, of self-promoting, worldly but working-class guy on the make, and third wheel who is more acted upon than is potent in the world—the classic schlemiel in protestant midwestern form—with a noirish, sexually hungry edge. "There's something about the sound of my own voice that fascinates me," he tells Mildred, and then, "With me being smart's a disease," both delivered with just the right amount of curdle—too much and he'd seem like the film's existential hero, a kind of supporting Phillip Marlowe without the gun; but Carson speaks his line with a light disdain, as though he's appreciating the bitter irony that he's the only audience for his own uniqueness with a glib nonchalance. It's a line delivery perfected by Eve Arden, who is, of course, also in Mildred Pierce, and with whom Carson has some scenes in passing.

They seem almost like gender-opposite twins who don't recognize each other, perhaps too much alike, but forlornly, it's hard to not feel, watching the two of them, that the verbal repartee creates a spark that would be fun to see really lit. Eve Arden, as Ida Corwin, seems to know this, but as happens with so many of Eve Arden's characters, as has happened to so many women, her wit and intelligence become desexualizing to the men around her (if not to us). She says after one encounter with Wally Fay (Jack Carson): "I'm getting tired of men talking to me man to man." But as if to match the gender inversion of the film's wittiest characters, Jack Carson becomes strangely feminized and infantilized; dressed in an apron at Mildred's restaurant, wanting an evening with Mildred, he comments, to Eve Arden no less, that all he was getting was "dish pan hands and a date with a Girl Scout [Mildred's daughter Vida, ironically the film's femme fatale]."

Jack Carson and Eve Arden were matched and again missed each other in the Carson-Doris Day vehicle, *My Dream Is Yours* (1949). *My Dream Is Yours* is much less than the sum of its parts: directed by Michael Curtiz, with songs by Harry Warren, Jack Carson has top billing among a cast of stellar character actors (Day, who was just beginning and whom Carson by all accounts mentored graciously throughout a two-year affair during which they made two of Day's first films, was to outshine her mentor's career immediately); the supporting cast includes Eve Arden, S. Z. Sakall, Edgar Kennedy in his last film, Franklin Pangborn (of whom more later), Adolphe Menjou, and Sheldon Leonard. A character-actors feast! The film is tolerable if one views it as a skipping stone from character actor to character actor bit. But it's a rather tired plot with Carson as a small time PR guy trying to get Doris Day noticed. What interests me is that here, again, there is that spark between Arden and Carson, both of whom know their way around a wisecrack, both of whom present as clearly secondary to Day, despite Carson's technical status as leading man; both Carson and Arden are characters who are too sexually denatured by their humor (yes, this happens to men, too, though male comic leads in other films sometimes "get the girl"—you need only look at the absurdly attractive wives of Laurel and Hardy in some of their films). But what's dreadful here is that Carson and Arden (their names sound good together—that sweet assonance) have an implied romance, but Carson and Day end up soaking Arden financially so Carson can promote Day, all while he's mooning after her, having apparently forgotten the romantic link to Arden. Can you say Nina Foch? You know I can. Arden, in short, gets used, and Carson gets the girl, completely unconvincingly, by a last-minute plot twist, in a kind of gesture of thanks for his devotion. Arden, we assume, gets paid back and invited to the wedding, having been made a fool of. Carson's character, like Arden's, is punished enough romantically in the film that we don't really resent him completely. It is Jack Carson, after all—there's some masochism built in. He's a nice, mostly transparent opportunist. And Doris Day is a sweet taker of everything that comes her way seems, well, just creepy. Perhaps she should have been paired with Gene Kelly's Jerry Mulligan in a kind of trans-filmic romance: *An American on the High Seas*. What bothers me most, as I said in the earlier essay, is that I associate Arden here with my pantheon of witty, sexual women who are absurdly, abjectly, and memorably discarded in favor of younger, usually blonder, and blander women: Eleanor Parker, Nina Foch, and Celeste Holm.

My Dream Is Yours is a disappointing failure because every-thing that happens that is at all interesting is on the margins, and the margins are marginalized by the dull story. It's like sitting around a dinner table with a group of wacky people and having the dull host remind you over and over of the occasion for the evening—his birthday. Carson isn't dull, but he's too earnestly yoked to plot; his role isn't to create disorder, which would suit his divisions and his sly *sotto voce* subversions, but order: get the girl (Doris Day) accepted by the world, which is a forgone conclusion.

Character actors who play leading roles usually only work with material refined for their specific talents and, even so, it can be thin gruel. A character actor, at her or his best, distills qualities fiercely, frequently taking her or his personae from film to film, with variations. But this distillation can also mean a somewhat narrower range and may work best in leading roles with characters who are robustly comic: Red Skelton or Danny Kaye, where there's shtick that can be elaborated to threaten real chaos. We recognize the Franklin Pangborn of Franklin Pangborn immediately, his proper, stuck up daffi-ness. Watching it for ninety minutes would be interminable. Enough Pangborn, we'd be driven to say, though it might be worth it just for the saying, as much as I love saying "Franklin Pangborn." "Cuddles" Sakall was charming in Casablanca, tending to Rick. But his Eastern European malaprops are amusing for about five minutes. Jack Carson only worked as the lead in light comedies like *Two Guys from Milwaukee*, the first of his films with pal Dennis Morgan, their lower-cost version of Hope-Crosby. In other films, *Arsenic and Old Lace*, *John Loves Mary*, *Love Crazy*, *The Strawberry Blonde*, and so on, he provided the comic relief of the funny second lead, or as a competing lover with the leading man. Jack Carson as a leading man who is too nice, not quite venal enough—for ninety minutes—falls headlong toward dull earnestness.

What makes Carson interesting elsewhere though, and is unusual for a character actor, is his unusual range and that touch of darkness in the soul, as he demonstrates in *Mildred Pierce*: the extension of his funny venality. Thelma Ritter, certainly in everyone's pantheon of character actors, was on the other side of this gravitas, having a light streak that tempered her moodiness. Some of the best character actors were extraordinary in their one-dimensionality: think about Mike Mazurki's big unforgettable brutes in films noirs, or Patsy's Kelly's great early sardonic maids. But some, like Carson and Ritter, pulled out surprising performances that stretched their essential screen personae, or even occasionally abandoned them. They were the rare character actors who performed both versions of possibility: they brought recognized personae from film to film frequently, and they also broke out to play well-defined and differentiated roles.

Carson did a couple of his strongest roles late: *Cat on a Hot Tin Roof* and *A Star Is Born*. In *Cat on a Hot Tin Roof*, directed by Peter Brooks and starring, of course, Paul Newman, Elizabeth Taylor and Burl Ives recreating his role from Tennessee Williams's Broadway play, Jack Carson plays Gooper Pollitt, Newman's brother. Gooper is the older brother, the one who's played it, well, straight: stayed home, married and procreated, went to law school, and has bided his time for his daddy's inheritance. He thinks he's played by the rules, and he wants his payoff. Jack Carson abandons his double takes for a character who is split emotionally: he wants his due, but he can't abandon his emotional sympathies for his younger brother. As played by Carson, who always brought a guilty mien to his more lighthearted guile, Gooper constantly sweats his double consciousness, his desire to inherit and his desire to do the right thing: to surpass his narrow interests. But unlike many of his earlier roles, Gooper is a conformist, and a man of intensely repressed feeling.

Jack Carson's performance as Matt Libby in the 1954 *A Star Is Born*, starring Judy Garland and James Mason (Carson had an impressive third billing), is one of my favorites of his and perhaps the best remembered after *Mildred Pierce*. Here, he demonstrates one of the virtues of a strong character: the ability to make an enduring impression with limited screen time. (Beatrice Straight is in everyone's Hall of Fame for having won the Academy Award for Best Supporting Actor, playing William Holden's wife in *Network* with five minutes and two seconds of screen time, dominated by one stirring scene in which she defines the pathos and fury of a betrayed spouse.) Carson has several scenes in the three-hour *A Star Is Born*, and he complicates the film in a way that I have always found *necessary* and manages to counterbalance James Mason's strongly unappealing performance as a bathetic, fame-benighted, alcoholic Pygmalion to Judy Garland's Galatea. Well, as they say, it's complicated. Mason urges Garland toward the fame he despises in a form that resists artificial makeovers (though this is in itself his pitch to sculpting her). In this way the film tries to keep him just this side of sympathetic, though I must say, as much I like James Mason and admire his performance, I have never found Norman Main, his character, sympathetic. In this, I am in agreement with Jack Carson's Libby, who despises him, and perhaps some credit is due to Carson's performance in convincing me of this opinion.

Libby is a flak hack, the studio press agent who represents Norman Main and tries to keep his reputation clean, despite his penchant for bad behavior, self-indulgent, whiskey-soaked, embarrassing escapades. In one symbolic episode early in the film, Main (Mason) accidentally throws Libby (Carson) through a mirror as Libby tries to prevent him from making a public jerk of himself at a movie premiere. Libby, the press agent, the stand-in for the studio's galaxy of stars, has a clear-eyed and cynical view of Main from the start. Carson says, in his best sarcastic delivery, "Mr. Main's charm escapes me. Always has." If Norman Main is the handsome romantic shell, Carson's Libby provides the alternative: big, bland looking, cynically realistic. And for my money, Carson makes the cynical realism seem much more appealing than Norman Main's self-destructive and narcissistic idealism, despite, as usual, a Carson-fissure, a note of slightly distasteful schadenfreude that seeps from Libby's pores during Main's downfall: he likes seeing the star he's had to cover and shill for go down the drain. But for me this makes Carson's Libby all the more believable and a truer counterbalance to the hollow romanticism of James Mason's Main. Judy Garland is the *sacre coeur* poised between the two, romantically somehow real and unembittered.

When Libby says he's been, too many times, "double-crossed by a cruddy actor," Moss Hart and Dorothy Parker—screenwriters separated by a generation—have found the right voice for a brilliant inside joke: it's bad enough to be betrayed, double-crossed in noir terms, but by a "cruddy actor" is comedy, a Hollywood punchline. And Jack Carson, a note of slight pain in his furrowed brow signifying what he's not gotten or what he's gotten wrong, what he hasn't solved or resolved in himself that would allow the world to make sense, makes this line bitter and funny in a way that few other actors could.

He was forty-four and would live nine more years. His last line in *A Star Is Born*, alluding to Norman Main's sacrificial suicide (the self-involved starfisher king?), is from Eliot's "The Hollow Men": "That's the way the world ends/Not with a bang, but with a whimper." Cosmological comedy—sardonic and funny—poetry as existential wisecrack. The end of character.

COMEDY AND PAIN

ERIC BLORE, WITH A SIDE OF FRANKLIN PANGBORN

Eric Blore was born in Middlesex in 1887, and he began his professional life as an insurance agent, which makes perfect physiognomic sense—he *looks* like an insurance agent. He also looks very much like the roles that came to dominate his ninety or so film credits: butlers and valets, headwaiters and hotel managers, men who serve in some capacity. I suppose I'm saying that butlers look like insurance agents, which I've never quite considered, but now that I do consider, it has the ring of absolute truth, or, at the very least, mild plausibility or, as Robert Benchley might have said, but perhaps would have restrained from saying, errant possibility.

Eric Blore is certainly the *name* of a character actor, the producers-that-be never bothering to change it, never needing to, which is true, as well, for the names of many other character actors (for instance, Franklin Pangborn) by the same reasoning that they *did* change the names of their leading actors: character actors could have names with character, suggesting quirks

11. Eric Blore. Wallofcelebrities.com.

12. Franklin Pangborn. Historic
Collection / Alamy Stock Photo.

or strangeness, even, at times, ethnic connections, whereas leading actors, the Issur Danielovitch Demskys (Kirk Douglas), William Beedle Jrs. (William Holden), Natalia Zakharenkos (Natalie Wood), and Doris Kapelhoffs (Doris Day) had to be smoothed out, WASPed, for a general audience.

Eric Blore, clearly enough, is just a letter, an inflection away from "bore," and the consonantly traffic jam of *c* and *b* suggests trouble. Franklin Pangborn is an entirely different matter. Pangborn sounds like either some kind of comically emotional ricochet, as in, "I barely had time to register my sorrow before I was pangborned into laughing at my own absurdity," or an Old English anachronism for a difficult birth: "âgnod hêahmægenûteweard wanspêdig cwên tôhwon bêgra pangborn." But in both men we have names suited for a character actor, and a specifically comedic one at that: yet another example of my long-held belief in nominal determinism.

The two actors shared this: born two years apart (Pangborn in 1889, Blore two years earlier), they both served in the First World War. Blore was with the South Wales Borderers, and though not much more is known about his service, the probability that he saw combat is likely. Pangborn, on the American side, was in the infantry and was gassed and wounded at the Battle of Argonne. Both men frequently played characters easily frustrated, with short fuses.

Why Eric Blore specifically interests me (though Franklin Pangborn, too—as often as I get a chance to pronounce his name I will, simply for the delight, the balanced syllables and the imbalanced sense—the stolid Franklin, and the silly Pangborn, the setup and the punchline, the step and the banana peel: Pangborn is a nominal banana peel) is what I want to think about, because I think Blore connects both to something in me and in comedy that I want to understand. Clearly, at some point, either Fred Astaire, who had worked with him on the *Gay Divorce* on Broadway or Mark Sandrich, who directed many of the Astaire-Rogers films, noticed his particular talents and started casting him over and over in the Astaire-Rogers films, more appearances as a character actor than any other—more even than Edward Everett Horton, his best foil. And this both springboarded and typecast Blore— although not completely—as the supercilious but frustrated butler or valet or waiter, the under-class role of the hyper-solicitous subordinate with a cultivated servant's English accent, clearly more refined than his American employers (though his own class provenance was frequently dubious in the films).

What is so funny about Blore, but also so interesting? For me, it's the quickness of his veering from delight to pain. He is delighted when, as a corrective, describing exactly how things should be done, or offering a finicky, minute bit of protocol. He seems to love talking about these things the way an antiquarian does with arcana. He has a bit of knowledge that no one is interested in and he wraps the extravagance of his belabored accent around his knowledge like a tongue with its favorite succulence, speaking as though his audience were slow, etiquette-challenged. They are, of course, you see: Americans. But no one much cares about what he cares about, or his service, except to take it for granted. His scenes with Horton are many of his best, are riots of class inversion, and almost invariably the funniest in the films of Astaire and Rogers that they're in together.

Blore's pain is almost invariably based on miscommunication, on misunderstandings of pronunciation, on the exactitude of diction (his) that others mangle or mishear, and his insistence on forms of behavior that fit the decorum of situations that his masters, the men he serves specifically or generally ("butling" them or serving them in restaurants, hotels) seem intent on violating. Which is to say, Blore always seems to come from a place where knowledge is settled—an historically accepted decorum—even though relational hierarchies are wavering, empires are crumbling, it's the middle of the Depression, and this is the United States, not England.

Blore's most famous line, repeated in two films (first in *The Sky's the Limit* [1943], another Fred Astaire film, sans Ginger), was: "If I weren't a gentleman's gentleman, I could be such a cad's cad." Blore's performances all smack of farce, of the drawing room, with the attendant suggestion of mistaken identity, with a wash of modern absurdity and class consciousness thrown in. *Is* he a cad's cad? In *Top Hat* (1935), the most successful of Astaire and Rogers's films (and RKO's most profitable film of the 1930s), Blore is the valet to Edward Everett Horton, though we hear right off the bat that the two are in a struggle—an unconventional relationship, certainly—when Horton (as Horace Hardwick) tells Fred Astaire (Jerry Travers), "My man Bates . . . we've had a bit of a tiff." He goes on to explain that "Bates is never right," a curious assertion toward the man charged with dressing him and generally arranging his household affairs. Their disagreement, which has all the hallmarks of a domestic spat, a couple's quarrel, is over Horton's ties, the use and selection of which Blore disapproves. Upon meeting Astaire, Blore says, "Allow us to introduce ourselves, sir. We are Bates." The hilarious pomposity of the royal "we," its grandiosity, further reinforces the sense that in the coupling of Horton-Blore, Blore sees himself as the superior partner. His English royal "we" trumps the sickly, sloppy American "I." Bates is slumming by serving a "master," whose haberdashery is clearly so unrefined, so chaotic.

But there's more: we learn in an important aside between Astaire and Horton what Bates-Blore's provenance is. He's been hired from the Salvation Army. So he is a butler hired out of hard times—can you say *My Man Godfrey*, filmed the following year. (This is the Depression, after all, and part of the success of Astaire and Rogers is the glamour of their films and the escapism associated with Astaire's tuxedo and top hat; although too infrequently does it get marked that the Depression either appears around the edges of the films themselves, or that Astaire in many of the films is marked as humble in origins, a hoofer, a vaudevillian, who then scores some kind of big success.) Six years later, Eric Blore (and Franklin Pangborn!) features as the valet in Preston Sturges's *Sullivan's Travels*, which has an opposite class trajectory: the wealthy director moving downward to try and experience (absurdly) the life of the lower class. But to the point: Blore's hyperconscious language, his super-sibilant butler's compensatory hyperarticulation, which would never work in an English setting (he would be seen as social climbing and absurd, and dismissed for being florid, rather than . . . serviceable) suggests that he has, at some point, had a reasonable position and, well, slipped, fell through the economic cracks. The Englishness of his gentleman's gentlemanliness, his recent status as discarded, the bickering relationship with his master all conspire to create class confusion, instability, a petri dish of chaotic elements from which comic situations can grow.

At the end of *Top Hat*, Blore-Bates, having served his "masters" through a series of madcap misadventures that push the

Astaire-Rogers film close to musical screwball comedy at times, finds himself soaking wet as a debunked gondolier and facing a poker-faced carabiniere who finds his imposture actionable, and what's more, unamusing. Bates, for all his loyalty, his service, is going to be arrested. Faced with this implacable countenance and the opportunity for a free pass to express his resentment of authority, he says, "You don't understand English? I've been waiting for an opportunity like this since my childhood, you frozen faced flatfoot." The carabiniere, obligingly, replies, "Grazie, signore." Bates-Blore, assured that he can continue to express his resentment, proceeds with relish: "Grazie to you, you stultified shrimp. Can I help it if you look like a mildewed donkey? Oh, I'm adoring this." On cue, the carabiniere: "Grazie, signore." Continuing: "And grazie to you, since you insist; you see I happen to be breaking the law; I admit it wholeheartedly, but of course you would never know that, you fish-faced nincompoop."

"Grazie, signore."

Laughing, Bates says goodnight and turns to leave, at which point the carabiniere, in perfectly accented, though uninflected English, reads him an arrest warrant. Blore's face squeezes in comic consternation while an eyebrow rises at the risibility of the subterfuge and the strange absurdity of the scene we and he have witnessed.

Blore was a master at prefulmination, something headed way past exasperation and frustration. His face became a kind of volcanic surface when he was annoyed, eyes darkly narrowed, and his lips would bubble like hot lava. You knew he would soon say, "Sir," or, "Excuse me," in the tone of a servant wanting to make an arrest but knowing, of course, that despite having the high ground (the sense of knowledge, of protocol—the right tie to wear, who should be in whose room), despite being on the edge of high dudgeon, he lacked the "law" behind him: he was merely right; he was trying to enforce the class rules he inherited onto the class he served, who sometimes just didn't care about the rules, thus, Edward Everett Horton wearing the wrong tie. One of the things that interests me most about Blore is how often in his central performances—and here I mean *Top Hat, Shall We Dance, The Lady Eve*—Blore either runs afoul of the law or is on the wrong side of it. His serving the interests of the upper class don't seem to serve him particularly well in *Top Hat* and *Shall We Dance*, and in Preston Sturges's *The Lady Eve*, which I'll talk more about later, he's an out-and-out swindler, a delighted parasite on the wealth of suburban Connecticut, trading on the American upper class love of aristocracy, especially English. If his accent allows him to bully Americans with a confusion about his class origins, despite his status as servant, in *The Lady Eve* it is Americans' self-duplicity in the desire to undemocratically throw themselves at Sir Alfred McGlennan Keith, a clearly Scottish name that doesn't in any way jibe with Blore's accent or presentation that serves as parody of the pretensions of class.

But I want to talk about *Top Hat* and *Shall We Dance* a bit more, where Blore's performances seem so, well, painful, at times. So pained really. Of course it's comic, comedic pain, and this is part of the great source of its power. The standard line about comedians is about how often their work is rooted in anger, and that the source of anger is some kind of enabling wound. But comic character actors are different from comedians—their essences are performative and expressive as opposed to the writerly source of comedians. Comedians may be fine performers, too, of course, and their sense of performative timing is crucial to the delivery of their material—most of us have had the experience of seeing/hearing material that was really good, but not particularly well delivered. The water used to be more muddied in the division between comedian and comic character actor than it is now, when comedians, in vaudeville, on radio, and early TV, had bits of their own but frequently relied on shifting teams of writers and existed less on the strength of wildly original material, as most of today's comedians do, than on the uniqueness of persona and acuteness of comic timing. Think Jack Benny, Bob Hope, Buddy Hackett, all of whom were extraordinary character actors in film.

The now familiar bromide that comedy is tragedy plus time, repeated pedantically by Alan Alda in Woody Allen's *Crimes and Misdemeanors* as though this were his original thought, has been attributed to various people, from Lenny Bruce to Carol Burnett to Steve Allen, but it seems Mark Twain was really the first to say it, or some version of it. He also wrote, in *Following the Equator*, that "the secret source of humor itself is not joy, but sorrow." I'd widen that: I'd say comedy is also about complication, error, misrecognition, dissatisfaction—yes, and sometimes a wellspring of hot underground misery or tragedy that needs to lose its heat as it approaches the surface and cools into humor. Comedy helps us face taboo, the unspeakable, the repressed, the heartbreakingly irresolvable, through transmutation into supposedly safer territory. But comedy is frequently therefore a veneer allowing the articulation of "dangerous" ideas, feelings, situations: think of the comedy of mistaken identification from Greek theater with its masks, to Shakespeare's comedies, and so on: Restoration comedy, the parlor comedies of (un)revealed affiliation and the way they more than flirt with incest, the graveyard jokes covering the existential skulls and bones of the gravedigger, children's delight in ghastly jokes of blood and mayhem (some of these hang around for generations), what we call "black humor," merely a stroke away from much of the rest of jokes we tell, in fact, but consigned to a special category we lower our voices for because we need to qualify our delight in the grotesque, the misshapen punchline that renders a deeply satisfying groan from our listener, as though we had violated their deepest sense of decorum, but they could only hope for more. The essence of comedy is repackaging the painful; however one might style "pain."

But Blore. You might wonder why I'm writing about a man who played fussy butlers, stuttering valets. Why *him*? Maybe the key to all of his performances is actually in *Fancy Pants* (1950), with Bob Hope and Lucille Ball. *Fancy Pants* is one of Blore's last significant roles. He's only fifty-three, but seems older, and is playing a dual role that is both extraordinarily funny and rather haunting. True to many of his performances, all of *Fancy Pants* is about class, inversions of roles, masquerade. Bob Hope plays an actor who onstage, in England, is playing an American butler impersonating (badly) an English butler. Blore plays, variously, (he is acting in both his onstage and offstage roles in the film) a member of the same company as Hope and then an aristocratic gentleman who Hope's faux gentleman's gentleman is masquerading as to curry favor with the rough mannered but financially endowed American, Lucille Ball. Got that straight? It's like a funhouse, B-movie comedy Henry James. Without—you know—all the pratfalls.

But what's so uncannily funny about Blore, whose trademark

was always his slippery butler's accent and his linguistic duel with American slang, is that he's completely unintelligible throughout the film. Not to put too Monty Pythonish a spin on it, but he really does sound like a stroke victim who doesn't know he's afflicted—an upper-class English accent rendered as a man speaking with a mouth full of marbles, unaware that his words, or perhaps any words, should have shape. Despite the film's mediocrity, it's a stroke of genius because of the way Blore's incomprehensible speech (which Bob Hope translates, we guess as saying whatever he wants him to say) comments on how any British accent heard by class-climbing Americans, even one rendered as garbled and guttural nonsense, will be beaten into some kind of sense, respected as meaningful by the upwardly mobile. It's an Edward Learian premise with an Orwellian edge. Bob Hope's poker-faced interpretations of the unintelligible garble, with barely a wink to the fourth wall, to those of us wondering what strange language, really, Eric Blore is talking now that he isn't serving badinage to Edward Everett Horton, are the meat grinder through which the colony puts the language of the "mother country."

This anarchistic, postcolonial flirtation is actually dangerous territory for a mild comedy on the cusp of the 1950s with no obviously larger satirical end in mind. (Bob's Hope brilliance was in the moment, the aside, the prefiguring of the anxious unmasculine man who managed to make stolid patriarchal figures look ridiculous—that's one of the reasons he and Jack Benny and Red Skelton were so influential on the generation of comedians who followed them. But then again, haven't male comic figures—the jester—always been something of a thorn in the side of the patriarchy? I always found it amusing when a comic's anarchy turned into an older comedian swinging a golf club and speaking at the Republican convention. Shout out to Groucho for never having fallen victim to that.)

So, in *Fancy Pants*, Eric Blore, the paterfamilias Sir Wembley (who, again, is *not* Sir Wembley but an actor playing him, and is equally incomprehensible in *any* role he plays), shows us how in his roles the figure of English decorum has progressed: from a post–World War I figure of ridiculous and dubious gentility (the *gentleman's gentleman*) to a post–World War II figure of raving incoherence—that's the way the world goes, from mild nonsense to insane blather. What makes it constantly funny (uneasily, again, since it has the whiff of disability, or madness) is that no one really seems to notice. Imagine hearing the most twee British accent: "Oh dear old Daddy. No one has ever really been able to figure out anything he's saying." (My interpolation.)

A film that once again demolishes assumptions about class but uses Eric Blore as a wrecking ball, rather than a chess piece, is Preston Sturges's *The Lady Eve* (1941), one of the great American comedies and an essential screwball. Blore plays one of the many grifters in the film (including Eve [Barbara Stanwyck]) who have their eyes out for moneyed pigeons to pluck. Curly, Blore's "real name" in the film (he has almost no hair), seems either ironic (Three Stooges) or a nod to a knowledge of earlier physiognomy and is used sparingly by his grifter friends. He has taken on the absurdly titled pseudonym of Sir Alfred McGlennan Keith—absurd because the Scottish name ill suits his utter Englishness, but if you're going to pull a con, why not just go over the top, pay no attention to logic. As Curly says to his con men and women friends of his marks among the moneyed American class, "When one's name is Sir Alfred McGlennan Keith, RFD [an invented

acronym—Royal Fire Department? Royal Forensic Duelists?]
one doesn't have to meet them, one fights them off with sticks.
And there's no hurry, we have them through the year, like a
lease." Blore-Curly's casual disdain for the American upper
class of Connecticut, and their swooning for his aristocratic
pedigree, is as pleased and unfraught as any overmatched meeting between hunter and prey. It's delightfully cynical. Asked if
he knows the wealthy beer baron Pikes, the family of Henry
Fonda, whom Barbara Stanwyck has courted and been thrown
over by, Blore says, "Do I know them? I positively swill in their
ale." With Preston Sturges, Blore trades his fluster for bluster,
of a rather cool kind. But he's still all about the confusions of
class, the mistaking of an accent and look for the supposedly
genuine article. But of course anyone and anything interested
in satirizing the noblesse oblige and those who would enshrine
it, understands that the emptiness of privilege is to demon-
strate how its manners are mannerisms and that its decorum
is merely decorous. As Orson Welles so brilliantly reminds
us in *F for Fake*, copies can not only pass for the original but
actually be more interesting. Blore, whether talking up to his
"masters" as butler, and befuddling them, or talking down to
the admirers of his faux aristocratic bona fides, is a sibilant
sibyl of the American ideology of anti-aristocracy—his role
is to show how artificial the rules of politesse are, and how
manners are merely constructs. We are meant to understand
that he's *here* because he doesn't want to, or simply can't, be
there. Thus, slumming, and suggesting the entire idea of class
is rather surreal. Eric Blore (Eric Blair?) in his own way is a
comic force for democratic populism.

If it isn't already clear, what I love about Eric Blore's characters are their pained attempts to serve and maintain dignity, to

convey what they believe are the proper forms, to use language in ways that are specific, pleasing, but that create ideological friction. He veers from frustration into moments of delight, which I must confess my complete identification with. When he breaks through to seeming communication, acknowledging the point with a "Yes" (whose final consonant can last weeks), there is a palpable relief, a lift of anxiety that I feel with him, as though a simple resolution were the impossible chalice that anyone could spend a lifetime trying to track. For someone as conflict averse as I consider myself, during these moments of relief, the bliss lighting up his face almost bizarrely beatific, I simply experience Blore as an icon of misunderstanding (or: a martyr?) and its attendant near miss: misery.

Take this interchange with Edward Everett Horton in *Gay Divorcee* (1934), the second Astaire-Rogers film, in which Blore recreates the role of the Waiter, which he first played on stage with Astaire. Serving Everett Horton, he asks, "Would you be the kind of man who would ring for a toasted scone?" Everett Horton, in his continuing role of befuddled and neurotic Yankee, for whom language is full of trap doors, is perpetually annoyed by Blore's characters in all their mutual screen appearances. He replies, "No, no, try me again."

Blore: "Can you imagine yourself with a hankering for a nice gooseberry tart?" (His questions, *are you the kind of man*, *can you imagine yourself*, asking so much more of Everett Horton as patron in a restaurant than he is prepared for.)

Everett Horton: "No, no what an acid thought."

Blore: "No crumpets, no gooseberry tart?" He seems perturbed.

Blore: "Well, that lands both of us in the cul-de-sac. You know, I hate to leave both of us like this. You torn with doubt and me with my duty undischarged. . . . Now sir, was it a bit of half-and-half? A noggin of ale, a pipkin of porter, a stoop of stout, or a breaker of beer?" Here, Blore gleams, he is shining with self-delight. And despite Everett Horton's attempts to regain his equilibrium, perhaps his mastery, by asserting his desire, simply, for tea, as a deflating riposte, Blore's delight will not be undone. "Tea?" he says. "Well, isn't it a small world, sir!" In short, tea is English, and no matter who is master, in the world of tea, Blore, though he serves, is no spiritual underling. This moment is full of the sparks of empire, or perhaps it's the embers. Which is no doubt why all Everett Horton can do is respond with one of his masterful double takes.

Perhaps you thought I'd forgotten about Franklin Pangborn? It's been pages and pages since I've crossed my eyes with delight at his nominal tensions (can a *Franklin* be a *Pangborn*? Should he? Where have all the Pangborns gone? Etc.), his oxymoronic name. But I haven't forgotten. Pangborn appeared with Blore in Preston Sturges's *Sullivan's Travels*, and occupies a special place in the heart of devotees of character actors. Pangborn, with Blore, played men who serve (remember, ironically they both "served" in the worst of circumstances, in World War I—did that give their performances as underlings a twist, an unstated frisson of exasperation?) though Pangborn's specialty was managers of various kinds: bank assistant managers, hotel managers, nightclub managers. But frequently he was second in charge, at best. And the role of "assistant" manager is important to note since it adds an extra layer of vexation to his scenes, those moments when one is thwarted but lacks a complete control of one's environment.

I always associated with those frustrated representatives

of authority, those butlers and assistant managers, Blore and Pangborn, not because I associated with authority but with resistance to it, because their roles themselves represent men who have become caught in a process or organization, acting out of duty in a way that inevitably leads to frustration.

When a good-looking hero flaunts the rules with a bit of delightful, minor anarchy (brings a woman into his chambers for the night, takes what he needs for the moment without paying for it, simply acts based on what he wants in situ—leading-men roles in many Hollywood golden era comedies are really big babies with uncontrollable ids) I was and still am torn in my reaction. I enjoy the anarchy, the rules broken—how could I not, having gone to late-night school with the Marx Brothers for so long—but another part of me, and I think perhaps many viewers, also feels the pathos in the comedy of the clerk, the butler, the assistant manager who is befuddled, irritated, confused, overruled in his (or her, of course, though policing characters tend more often to be male) attempt to play by or enforce the rules, because they have to, because they've learned that that's their role, that's how they get by. Chaos is the fantasy of our childhoods, and the liberated occasional moments of our adult lives, so it makes sense that leading men and women, within the bounds of the Code, can take liberties with behavioral delinquencies (as long as they don't really challenge the social order). But leading actors in their roles almost always end up supporting conventional patterns of behavior, despite their flouting moments.

It is the strange intensity of the comically straightlaced service figure, like Blore and Pangborn, that ends up, ironically, seeming more challenging, even borderline transgressive. Think of Blore's "stroke" dialogues, the class inversions in his roles.

With Pangborn, early on, the ease with which he was provoked into a kind of male hysteria raises all kinds of subtle questions about gender, sexuality, control. Gradually, the comic element in his career became explicitly about when he would be provoked into an almost surreal, manic crisis. Man crisis.

Pangborn's face is bulldog rectitude with a pencil moustache. Before he is thwarted he usually smiles with a winning and disingenuous sense of barely contained servitude. Maybe that's why Pangborn was always so funny—the secret of his officiousness was his simultaneous commitment to it and undermining of it, and the sense, in his face, that the function of the functionary was beyond dutiful, was almost hieratic, and personally painful. When, inevitably, the ordinary run of things was disturbed, when for example, he was charged in Preston Sturges's *Hail the Conquering Hero* with arranging the heroic interludes of music hailing faux hero Woodrow Lafayette Pershing Truesmith (Eddie Bracken), only to have his student bands inevitably start playing at the wrong moment. ("Not yet, not yet!" he keeps imploring, as though the war, II, were being lost because of a few stray notes, loose trumpet lips sinking ships.) Pangborn becomes desperate. His slicked-down hair starts to commit civil disobedience; his narrow eyes widen and dart with panic.

And his voice: Pangborn, though born in New Jersey, was one of many first generation talkie actors who possessed or nurtured a high culture New England or Mid-Atlantic accent (Edward Everett Horton had this, too), which was like an English accent that had been through a cycle of the wash, probably cold. I'm not sure that this accent exists in the United States anymore, but you hear it everywhere in films of the '30s and, to some extent, the '40s (I think the war might have dried it out). It was a remnant of a time when accent and class were more linked than they are now in the United States. The easiest way to signify education, or power, or the upper class, was to have a character speak as though they had been through Harvard but docked at Southampton.

When Pangborn loses his wits because things aren't going his way, his voice rises, and he starts to act like a windup toy bumping into walls, turning this way and that, not knowing what to do with his body now that the rules are being broken, now that the world isn't working exactly the way he was told it should. He's a funny little priest who can't remember who his god is. In other words, he breaks down. And it's painfully funny. No one has ever been better than Pangborn (can we create a Nominal Hall of Fame and start it off with "Pangborn," "because once said, it must be repeated"?) at showing us that bureaucracy's front man is not only vulnerable but close to hysterical.

Blore and Pangborn were two of the best of the many footmen and servitors, majordomos and stewards, middlemen and supervisors who show up in Hollywood film. In comedies that try to find a footing to represent or, even in the rare case of a more radical director like Preston Sturges, undermine the complexities of American capitalist hierarchies—bosses and workmen, guests and waiters and waitresses, butlers and their "masters"—both actors always seem to be placed in situations that either cannot sensibly work for who they are or cannot work at all if you want to follow the rules. Their accented frenzies and implosions are, for me, always beautifully timed reminders of American social systems, stratifications not really so far gone from us, when this thing called "order" was just waiting to implode, before it started to explode.

MA

FIVE MOVIE MOTHERS, WITH A CODA ON HITCHCOCK

> This essay is about five movie mothers: Anne Revere (*Gentleman's Agreement*), Thelma Ritter (*Birdman of Alcatraz*), Elizabeth Wilson (*The Graduate* and *Little Murders*), Jane Darwell (*Grapes of Wrath*), and Margaret Wycherly (*White Heat*).

I take my mothers where I find them.

My ideas about mothers were formed early, on smallish, square screens, where I would watch both idealized and complicated mothers minister to idealized and complicated sons. Measuring myself and my own mother against them was a complex transaction. I had no idealized version of myself—but I think I had very early complications in my ego development. That is to say, my self-narrative began when I was seven or so, and I had a sense of, or believed in, its individuality, which wrapped around my feelings of empathy and woundedness, creating a primitive story of a kind of shipwrecked boy who was as threatened by inescapable maternal gravitation as by the unpredictable solar flares of paternal heat that seemed to augur an end to all life on earth, which was me. But if the patriarchy of my homelife was occasionally apocalyptic (and, in truth, occasionally charming and filled with moments of generosity, as well; how much easier *everything* would be if our

13. Anne Revere. Wallofcelebrities.com.

14. Thelma Ritter. Wikimedia Commons.

15. Margaret Wycherly. Library of Congress, George Grantham Bain Collection.

16. Jane Darwell. Wallofcelebrities.com.

17. Elizabeth Wilson in *The Graduate* (1967), with Dustin Hoffman.

18. Elizabeth Wilson. Wallofcelebrities.com.

statements could be pure, simple, or "pure and easy," as Pete Townsend put it) it was still, ironically, more limited. I really grew up in a maternal (if not matriarchal) world—the world of my mother and grandmother, who lived in the bottom half of our row house and with whom I shared a bed for two years—for most of my days and evenings. And so I have always been attuned to mothers, to women, then, I think, and now. And some of the mothers I first watched in my childhood—child of the movies that I was—stay with me. And I want to think about why some of these specifically different models have stayed with me for so long, these archetypes of the forgiving, embracing, crazed and bizarre mothers.

I dreamt last night that I was in a concentration camp—I'm not making this up. I was with a group that veered from being family to people I barely knew—symbolic enough in itself—and then there were two women, one older, and one younger, and both were posed in the dream as romantic interests (yes, even in my concentration camp dreams I have romantic "interests"—a cinematic term), but for once I wasn't interested, well perhaps a little abstractedly in the younger woman, who seemed sad and distracted (perhaps narcissistically, I've always been attracted to people with wounds). An old man gave each of us amulets, pieces of metal and glass that were meant to help save us, "when the time comes." But when I woke up I thought about how helpless the women in the dream were and then thought how having been born a scant decade after the end of the World War II, and surrounded by the aging refugees of what seemed like its far-off devastations, the world of my childhood was a combination of maternal safety and paternal anxiety. My mother could protect me at home, and my father made me anxious. (Though my father could also protect me, and did, from the wolves at the door—once, he literally chased a pack of dogs away from me!) But if it came down to it, neither would be much help against the forces that ravaged the old men and women on the Boardwalk at Brighton Beach, the camp survivors, whom I used to talk to, would look at me as they tanned on the boardwalk as though I were a strange little American creature; a little more than ten years after they were liberated from the camps. Ten years ago Obama was president. *The Fast and the Furious* came out. I always return to the movies, especially when I feel the cold touch of any kind of creeping anxiety.

The camps were liberated and then ten years later I was born. So I grew up with a heightened sense of the Holocaust, especially as a Jewish kid in New York. Everyone had relatives in Poland or Germany or Romania who did or didn't make it out. And because of the heightened awareness of the Holocaust, there was a renewed focus on anti-Semitism in the United States, aided by Laura Z. Hobson's bestselling book *Gentleman's Agreement*, which was published right after the war ended, in 1946. Darryl F. Zanuck bought the rights for the film after he was denied entry into the Los Angeles Country Club; they assumed (wrongly) he was Jewish. You know: Hollywood film producer, foreign-sounding name. Perhaps you know the film; it was a big hit: Academy Award for best film of the year in '47, best supporting actress for Celeste Holm, best director for Elia Kazan, along with a slew of other nominations, including Anne Revere for supporting actress. When I was growing up, and for years after, it carried the aura of the uber-"quality" film, a serious film, an issues film, and it was made by Kazan before his (for many of the left) self-immolating naming of names before HUAC, before the sellout that made it difficult to love his films without twists and turns of either hermeneutics or apologetics: *On the Waterfront* was secretly an apology (and the counter argument, that it was really an apologia for squawking to McCarthy and his kind), or *A Face in the Crowd* was atonement and the exposure of dangerous populism. We wanted to love Kazan, because we really did love these films, but we never found a way to. We really could never forgive him. This is called the road to endless rationalization, or perhaps just deciding what one, as a consumer of culture, can and cannot live with. The battles, internal and external, rage on: Polanski, Woody Allen, Riefenstahl . . .

But *Gentleman's Agreement*, coming before Kazan's original sin, was a film that, despite the fact that it's discursive and in many ways an inert film, we could embrace. More than anything else, it was *the* postwar film on anti-Semitism, and so, for those of us in the leftish, Jewish, baby boomer world of cinephilia, it had a place at the table.

The United States got pretty sleepy about anti-Semitism in the late twentieth century. And in these first two decades of the twenty-first, until, well, it became impossible to not wake up, as "Jews will not replace us" was chanted in Charlottesville, Jews were shot at a synagogue in Pittsburgh, and so on. But if you were paying attention, smaller-scale versions of these were happening for decades. I certainly grew up with anti-Semitism as a normal *thing*, even in New York, in Brooklyn, for god's sake, one of the largest Jewish cities in the world. I was egged coming out of Hebrew school, called every Jew derogatory name you can think of. And despite my uneasy distance from the Jewish world (some might question this) (*my sister, my daughter . . . my Jewishness, my distance*) I've been aware of it as a relatively constant accompaniment throughout my life. Through the years, when I would talk casually about anti-Semitism—you know, as the kind of patter one indulges in before a movie starts: "How's the new relationship? What's up at work? Why do they hate the Jews?"—I'd usually get a glazed over response, as though I were suddenly speaking in tongues, or Yiddish, or a particular brand of burnished cultural paranoia.

This is so painful I've only told a few people this story. I was in a bar in upstate New York, during graduate school. I always loved to go to the north side bars of Syracuse, which were Polish and Italian, old, and frequently pretty beat. I was at one on a Friday, a bar that business people went to after work, but I was early. The holy cocktail hour, four for me. A businessman and woman sat at the end of the bar, the only other patrons. Loudly, the guy said to his companion, "You know the difference between a Jew and a loaf of bread? The loaf of bread doesn't scream when you put it in the oven." I slid my drink down the bar at them and it hit theirs, like bar bowling. The guy said, "What the fuck," and got up, but I said, "Fuck you," and walked out past him. I'm all for symbolic gestures. But I'm rarely in the mood to get myself beaten up.

Once in a class I was teaching in Ohio, we were reading a story (could it have been Phillip Roth's "Conversion of the Jews"?) when a conversations about "Jews" started in the class. It was a novel experience. I was taken aback that these smart young liberal arts students, so ingenuous, didn't, for the most part, know what a Jew was. "Don't they mostly care about money," one of them asked. "Only when they don't have enough of it to pay their rent," I said.

I could go on (I'll go on). Some years ago, a woman I was in love with, and whose political fervor I greatly admired, used to doggedly insist that there was no widespread or systematic anti-Semitism in Europe. I was floored, almost exploded by this argument. I was never sure whether it was some willful fantasy of post-anti-Semitism, or just an expression of such extreme empathy with the cause of the Palestinians, which I share, taking all the oxygen out of possible Jewish empathy (not to mention the unfortunate collapsing of "Jewish" with "Israeli"). But let me not go any further down that road, or I fear I'll never make it to the movies, and I want to make it to the movies because my mother is waiting there for me, my mothers, or at least some plausible, or maybe I should say desirable, facsimiles.

The mother in *Gentleman's Agreement* is Ann Revere, playing the mother of Gregory Peck (Phillip Green) a reporter who is hired to do an expose on anti-Semitism and comes up with the brainstorm that he will do so by posing as a Jew. His title, "I Was Jewish for Six Months." OK: Oy. I must admit, it always sounds to me like a particularly tense episode of *Bar Mitzvah Undercover*. And then my favorite unintentionally funny line in the film (I really do like it, with caveats): Phil says, "It won't be the same, for sure. But it'll be close." Huh? This idea/attitude probably led to the well-intentioned but unfortunate "I was a Negro in the South for thirty days" in 1948 "expose," and the much more well-known *Black Like Me*, by John Howard Griffin. When confusion of empathy and sympathy blocks one's smarter impulses, we're left with wince-inducing, and all too often, soft-underbellied agitprop: I need to try to be you for your experience to be understood by people like me and people not like me.

Ahem, I don't think so. The heart may be in the right place (is it? Navigating around the pulsing ego.) but not the head: I think my sardonic tone is clear enough.

To confuse the issue, though: *Gentleman's Agreement* is a novel written by a Jew who was "passing." The others were acts of misguidedly inspired journalism. Art trying badly to imitate life.

On the issue of empathy, there is no complication for me in the role of Phil Green's (Gregory Peck's) mother in *Gentleman's Agreement*: Anne Revere, the first of my surrogate screen mothers that I want to talk about. She played lots of mothers: to Montgomery Clift in *A Place in the Sun*, to Elizabeth Taylor in *National Velvet*, to John Garfield in *Body and Soul*. In all of these performances some similarities come through: emotional restraint with barely concealed deep feeling, deep reserves of strength of character. (She seems softly unmovable, utterly incorruptible, as the House Un-American Activities Committee found when they called Revere to testify, and she refused; she was blacklisted and after *A Place in the Sun*, in 1951, didn't make a film for twenty years. She did, however, win the Tony for Best Actress in 1960, for *Toys in the Attic*.)

Revere seems tough; she tells Peck, "Sympathy, oh no," when he's going through a rough patch, but it's because she has a surfeit of it that she can deny it, and he and we know this, and it ends up being very moving, in the way that it was at the movies when characters who were full of emotion let it on and pulled back—you weren't supposed to be too emotionally explicit, but of course this is just another trope for sentiment in the films of classical Hollywood, and frequently it's sentimental in a way I still find moving. It helps that Moss Hart, who wrote the screenplay, gives Anne Revere sharp and direct lines that she can deliver with off the cuff, wisecracking believability. "Why, women will be thinking next, Phil," she tells her son, in a soft kick the pants about his astonishment that Kathy, the object of his affection, came up with the original idea for the anti-Semitism story.

I suppose, having lived without a mother essentially my entire adult life, what enshrines Revere most for me in *Gentleman's Agreement* is Anne Revere good naturedly cheering her son on by calling him a "dope" through the movie, those belittling endearments so tenderly familiar to me from my childhood (along, I might add, with belittling belittlements, also a tender memory, but from soreness).

Revere, "Ma," gets the first read of Phil Green's, Peck's, manuscript. A mother reading her son's work with passion and conviction, sitting there on the lightly used middle-class sofa. For me this is writer's catnip, a wish fulfilment of the highest order: not only a living mother, but a living mother who is your ace, your trusted reader, waiting to read this, your latest and invariably your best work, so she can tell you that your life, ultimately, has meaning. The catch, in the film, is that Ma has a heart problem. Too big a heart? When the angina hits, she says to Phil, "I never realized pain could be so sharp . . . come back and hold my hand." When my mother was diagnosed with cancer, in 1980, I came back almost without thinking—I moved back to New York from California to hold her hand. It's interesting to think now that I never entertained second thoughts about the move back to New York from my golden state of escape. At least this is the version I tell myself, sculpted out of the necessities of memory. I was indeed the dutiful son. I find what I think of as my youthful clarity almost unbearably dear. I hope, dear reader, you can excuse this transport of self-approval in my inner time machine.

Being moved by the political possibilities in her son, Gregory Peck's expose, in Phil Green's fine work, Anne Revere speaks her moving set piece of *Gentleman's Agreement*—stilted and still moving after seventy-two years. She says:

> I suddenly want to live to be very old. Maybe it won't be the American century after all, or the Russian century or the atomic century. Wouldn't it be wonderful, Phil, if it turned out to be everybody's century? When people all over the world, free people, found a way to live together. I'd like to be around to see some of that, even the beginning. I may stick around for quite awhile.

It's a paean to hope from a mother to a son.

Two years later Revere's film career was cut short by McCarthyism, and my mother married my father. But Revere still managed to thrive, on stage and TV, as a teacher. And she lived until 1990, ten years past my mother.

* * *

When I was very young I used to confuse Thelma Ritter and Lotte Lenya. I think they were names I heard often, icons in my household and other households of the '50s and '60s. Lenya, the great singer, performer, actress, and wife of Kurt Weill, now known mostly for her performance as spectre agent Rosa Klebb in *From Russia with Love*. More dedicated cinephiles may know her performance as Contessa Magda Terribili-Gonzales in *The Roman Spring of Mrs. Stone*. My confusion ended when I saw Lenya onstage in the original production of *Cabaret*, and I've always wondered if she felt as though she were acting in a dream, acting out her memories of Berlin in the '20s. I've had an early recording of *The Threepenny Opera* for many years, Lenya singing "Pirate Jenny," of course. My thoughts of her veer between her fierce song of revenge and, well, a knife in shoe chasing James Bond around a room trying to get his briefcase. In between is a vague memory of Frau-lein Schneider, my delighted, heady transport at *Cabaret* at eleven, Jill Haworth as Sally Bowles and Joel Grey just starting his long run as the MC. All of it put together by Hal Prince, who, strangely, has died the very day I write this, Prince, who concocted or guided so many of my early to mid-life delights: *Cabaret, Fiddler on the Roof, Company, Follies, Pacific Overtures, Candide, A Little Night Music, Sweeney Todd*—I mostly remember Lenya's genial Germanic sophistication from that performance of my youth, that sense of ruefulness, of experience telegraphed with just a word, a vowel. This she does in fact share with Thelma Ritter, perhaps the premier character actress of a certain kind of middle-aged woman for many people; some of her roles, perhaps many of them, mothers, others, helpers of a motherly sort (*All About Eve* or *Rear Window*), and other more raw roles that fit her sarcastic or sardonic delivery of what comes across as acrid experience but is rendered in a particularly lively, even whimsical way: she rarely seemed downtrodden, beaten. She was jaded but not jaundiced. There's a difference.

If I weren't writing about mothers here, I'd write about Ritter in *The Misfits*, a film I've both variously loved and found tedious and unwatchable over the years, depending on my age, my mood, the time of year, or perhaps my own "misfittedness." The about-to-die performances by Gable (especially) and

Monroe are constantly on the edge of breaking, or is it cracking, so it seems. And in the middle of it all (with Eli Wallach, an actor whose Actors' Studio hamminess I've never been able to take for very long) Ritter shows a restless sexual edge—in the way she moves, the way she looks out to the middle and far distances—that isn't in any of her other roles. I'm tempted to say she steals the movie, but the movie itself is so bleak that it's a cliché that buries itself.

Ritter speaks with a strong New York accent; it's crucial to everything she plays because she never loses it. In this she's a perfect surrogate for me: my mother, too, had a strong New York accent, more specifically Brooklyn, but we could never figure out how she got it. She was born and lived in Lakewood, New Jersey, for her early years, and moved to Brooklyn when she was a teenager, when most accents are already fully formed. Perhaps she was especially susceptible, wanted to fit in with the city girls around her in the early 1940s? Certainly my grandparents' heavily accented Russian-Ukrainian wasn't an influence, cast her own accent into a kind of free float. Did she, I wonder, go to see *Miracle on 34th Street* when it came out, in 1947? In the film, considered Thelma Ritter's breakthrough, the actress, though uncredited, is trying to buy a Christmas present for her child. When she can't find it at Macy's, Kris Kringle (Edmund Gwenn) tells her to go to Bamberger's, then (and in my childhood) Macy's direct commercial and near-geographical competitor, on 33rd Street, where my father had his office. I could imagine Ritter, with her thick New York accent, as my mother, tired and seeking out the Christmas (or more likely Hanukkah) toy that would delight, walking the streets I knew so well. It's Thelma Ritter who reports the new "angle" of sending customers to other stores for toys that Macy's doesn't have that moves the plot along and curries Kris Kringle's favor with Mr. Macy as a publicity ploy. The implicitly Jewish shopper sees how smart the smart enterprise in commercial generosity might be.

Ritter is tired in *Miracle on 34th Street*, a tired mom, and Ritter frequently seems tired, a bit worn out, worse for wear. In *Pickup on South Street*, one of her best, if less iconic roles, in which she plays a government informant and pickpocket, but with scruples that prove deadly, she says of herself to the tune of the song "Mam'selle" ("A small café mam'selle. . . . And yet I know too well / Some day you'll say goodbye"): "You seen an old clock running down?" That world weariness, if not always in that intensely a foreshadowing way, is there in all of Ritter's performances.

But the other mother performance of Ritter's I want to talk about, is an uncharacteristic and memorable one; she was nominated for one of her six Academy Awards for her performance as Burt Lancaster's mother in *Birdman of Alcatraz* (1962), directed by John Frankenheimer, despite the small amount of screen time, just ten and a half minutes. Perhaps only Beatrice Straight, who was nominated for *Network* with about seven minutes of screen time, did more with less. But Ritter was always indelible. The reason this mother-son relationship stays with viewers, and has personal resonance for me, is because of its intensity, its complexity, the neurotic Oedipal suggestiveness at its core, and the necessary betrayal by Burt Lancaster's Birdman (Robert Stroud, the real prisoner upon whom the film is based) of his mother, who wants him all to herself.

My own relationship to my mother, of whom I've written elsewhere, was too close in the years leading up to adolescence, pubescence, and I basked in the glory of her presence. Her aura seemed to calm any rising anxiety; I was sure it could soften the winds. But when I hit fourteen I broke violently away in the need to remake myself and create myself, and she seemed to never recover from it. For years, I felt as though I had killed her when she died several years later, and very young, of cancer. Before her death, a looming, brooding sadness became her frequent mien, and though that was, I think, largely because her children were leaving home, I still blamed myself exclusively for it.

In *Birdman of Alcatraz*, we see Lancaster as Stroud in jail almost immediately for manslaughter, then, enraged, pummeling a man who dared to handle a photograph of his mother. One of his cellmates comments, "What kind of nut are you, anyhow, just because he picked up a picture of your mama?" Lancaster's retort is instructive: "You ever mention my mother again, I'll kill you." At least he's direct.

Later in the film, after years in isolation in prison, Lancaster is befriended by a lonely woman who admires his work with birds and "proposes" a business venture. Smelling the budding romance, Ritter, who has spent years fighting for her son, getting his prison changed, his hanging commuted, tells her son to abandon the romance, which has become marital. She essentially says it's her or me, and Lancaster says, well, it's her. Ritter says she will never see him again, and Stroud's mother did exactly that. In the film, as an extra twist of the knife, Ritter tells the authorities that her son should never be released from prison (because that would mean consummation of his marriage? True horror.), that he's a danger and should be kept in prison for life. Betrayal as displaced love, forbidden love.

I remember my own mother's barely concealed fury when

I started seeing my first girlfriend, at seventeen. When she came to our row house in Brooklyn and went downstairs to my room with me, I could feel my mother's icy umbrage directed at Wendy, my girlfriend, and I was embarrassed by it. Then, in the one instant I can ever remember where my mother's behavior struck me a "creepy," she was driving the three of us back from my high school graduation, Wendy and I sitting in the back seat with my hand on her leg. It's not as though we had started copulating in front of my mother. If anything, the presence of my mother acted as a kind of sexual antifreeze for me, an erotic contraceptive . But my mother stared at me in the rearview mirror at one point and said, "I can see what you're doing, and you better stop it right now." I could only deny and demur, which were honest reactions, but I felt guilty nonetheless, ready to serve my time with only birds as company.

I'm reminded of those mothers in movies who suddenly become absurdly large, like the mother in Woody Allen's "Oedipus Wrecks" from *New York Stories* who appears in the sky over Manhattan, or Guy Maddin's mother in *My Winnipeg*, whose enlarged face peers in through the window of the moving train as he attempts to escape from the city and her orbit—she is looking into his psyche; both of these mothers, and my own, crossing boundaries and dominating the landscape.

The last shot of Ritter in *Birdman of Alcatraz* is of her devastated face, aware of the extent of her own betrayal but unable to do anything but register her grief and disappear from her son's life. My own mother's betrayal was through death; perhaps I didn't kill her, but however she left, I, like Stroud, still felt abandoned, imprisoned by loss.

* * *

While we're on the subject of difficult mothers and neurotic mother-son relationships, I must pay homage to a favorite: Margaret Wycherly (Ma Jarrett) as James Cagney's (Cody Jarrett) mother in *White Heat*. There's no moll like an old moll, and when the moll's a mom, what more could a psychopathic boy gangster want?

Cody Jarrett and Ma Jarrett have a close, trusting, warm relationship. Cody leads a gang of thieves—whom Ma accompanies—most, though not all of whom seem cowed by his murderous psychopathy. One of them comments, "All his life he just put out his hand, and there was Ma Jarrett." We see Ma minister to Cody's crippling headaches early in the film, Ma telling Cody, "Don't let them see you like that. It might give some of them ideas." Isn't that heartwarming? Don't you wish you had a mother who was working behind the scenes to make sure you weren't knocked off? We also learn, in an important and amusingly brief bit of exposition, that Cody's headaches began when he was a boy (might we posit around the age of puberty?), and he started faking headaches to get the attention he coveted from his mother. Over time, life imitating acting and transforming into psychosoma, the headaches became real and wildly disabling. Cagney, brilliant as Cody, whimpers and lets out small animal screams as he seems to be trying to tear his head off whenever one of his headaches takes him over.

And Ma supports Cody whenever he is flagging with her (and apocalyptically, at the end of the film, his) tagline, "Top of the world," a toast, an encouragement, a prediction of good things to come when Cody, her beloved son, will be the eminent success he's cut out to be. I remember my own mother trying to boost my brother and me, somewhat less memorably, with her youthful mantra: "Good better best, never let it rest, until the good is better, and the better is best." I liked the way it scanned, but . . . I would have been happier with the less-cheerleading "Top of the world." Plus my mother was rather helpless as the thugs of Brooklyn routinely had their way with me from the ages of eleven to fifteen. Maybe I should have faked headaches and screamed like a wild animal instead of just quietly suffering the vague malaise that caused our family doctor to put me on uppers (they called them vitamins for several months). How I would have liked to hear my soft mother say what crazy Ma Jarrett says to Cody about the gang member who has betrayed and replaced him while he's in prison: "Any time I can't handle his kind, I'll know I'm getting old. No one does what he's done to you, son, and gets away with it."

If Cody Jarrett is the antihero of *White Heat*, sympathetic simply because James Cagney plays him with such extravagantly, energetically cracked vim, regressive, narcissistic, cruel, but nevertheless a very sweet and devoted son; Margaret Wycherly's Ma Jarrett is a kind of antiheroine as she combines the apotheosis of hardboiled gangstress with tender maternal apothecary to the psychotic prodigal. They're the Bonnie and Clyde of a kid and his mom. She makes sure Cody gets his full share of the take of a job the gang pulls when Cody is sent down, and tells him, when she visits, "You'll be out soon. Back on top of the world." Was he *ever* on top of the world? In his devoted mother's eyes, yes: sticking up a bank, or planning the next job.

Right before my mother died, she asked to see some of my

poetry—I must have been twenty or twenty-one years old. I shudder to think of the juvenilia I showed her; I also think tenderly of the juvenilia I might have shown her. In any case, I remember so vividly her saying to me, "It's just so deep. I never knew you were so deep." I suppose if Cody was given height by Ma, put on the top, I was given that brief gift of my mother's sense of depth. I thought it was a sweet thing to say.

Ma Jarrett dies in *White Heat* while Cody is in prison, the information relayed to him via a kind of game of telephone, prisoner to prisoner, while the men are sitting at the chow hall. We don't hear what they're saying, just see the whisper being passed on, until it finally reaches James Cagney. Director Raoul Walsh and Cagney kept their plans for Cagney's reaction from most of the rest of the cast playing prisoners in the cafeteria; they wanted to keep Cagney's extreme response surprising. Cody takes a second to digest the news, a flicker of comprehension mixed with denial registering on his brow, and then, in one of Cagney's most famous scenes, he turns into a kind of wild animal of grief, first quietly repeating the word "dead," then whimpering/screaming, jumping on the table, and running and skidding on his chest. He runs toward the exit, and as though supernaturally powered by the grief, in a kind of *aristeia*, he turns into a Hector or Achilles at the walls of Death, punching four guards in succession who try to subdue him with clubs raised but fall in the face of his supernatural death-inspired power. O death. Walsh gives us Edmund O'Brien's wide-eyed reaction shots, as though he (standing in for us) had never seen such a thing, such a display. Cagney's tortured screams sound to me variously like "I love you" and "get me out," but they're twisted, not really coherent. Finally four men grab him and carry him away crying and woundedly howling. I'm not sure grief has ever been as powerfully represented on film.

When my father called to tell me of my mother's death, I too voiced the need for repetition, not saying "dead" but asking him, "What did you say?" though I had plainly heard him. Is there something about the finality of death that makes us automatically, almost autonomously try to delay by using language: say again? Say the word. I remember the scene in "Circe" in *Ulysses in Nighttown*, when Stephen Daedalus says, "Tell me the word, Mother?" asking for the magic of language to heal him. But of course the complications of maternal love are all over Joyce, as Stephen says in "Scylla and Charybdis," "*Amor matris*, subjective and objective genitive, may be the only true thing in life."

Movies and memory can run backward and forward in our minds, tapered by language that chases its own tail like a mother-hungry Tantalus.

* * *

If there is a quintessential mother in early to midcentury American cinema, perhaps it's Jane Darwell, remembered best for her Academy Award–winning performance as Ma Joad in *The Grapes of Wrath* (1940), directed by John Ford (in my early years, I called my own mother "Ma," so perhaps my own preference in this essay for mothers who are so called in movies). Henry Fonda insisted she be given the role. But at that point she was well on the way in her extraordinarily prolific career as a film actress, over 170 film appearances, dating from 1913 to 1967 (she's the old woman in the "Feed the Birds" number in *Mary Poppins*, at Walt Disney's request, her final role). She was a most prolific screen mother: Ma

James in *Jesse James*, "Ma" Jenny Grier in *The Oxbow Incident*, Ma Stone in *The Devil and Daniel Webster*, Ma Marine in *The Singing Marine* (!), Ma Donohue in *All through the Night*, and Mom in *She's a Sweetheart*, along with many others, including the grandmother roles she inevitably aged into.

I always think of *The Grapes of Wrath* and *The Wizard of Oz* (released the year before, 1939) as the two greatest "heartland" films, both responding in different ways to the Depression, capturing the tumult in the agrarian middle of the country. There is a geography, too, to Jane Darwell's ample body and tragic face, her eyes always looking like they're about to tell who next will die, what next will be lost (if you remember, Grampa and Grandma die on the trip west to California, and Tom Joad, who has just been released from prison, spends a good part of the film, before finally leaving the family for good at the end, skirting going back to jail). For a film so much about privation, Darwell's largeness somehow doesn't intrude—her haggardness shrinks her physically, while her largeness, well, *enlarges* her emotionally, suggests she's the center of the family, which is true, if not completely solid, intimated by her thin and wavering voice, which frequently has a touch of vibrato in it, as though she were constantly speaking a kind of midwestern elegy. These are bleak times when anything can happen.

Darwell's mettle as the moral compass of the film, for both Tom and us, shows up early in their reunion, when she says of the manslaughter charge that put him in prison, "I wished you hadn't done it, but you done what you had to do. I can't read no fault in you."

Throughout, she's the magnetic core of family, as my mother was. After my mother's death, my nuclear family fractured, never to unify again. In the forty-five years between my parents' deaths, we gathered once for Thanksgiving, at my insistence, in my house in the Midwest. That weekend is a vague phantasmagorical disaster in my mind, with a few charming moments. Even Darwell's Ur-maternal force field can barely, if at all, keep at bay the forces that will tear the family apart—death, poverty, the fateful lopsidedness of power—as the police pursue her son. Remembering the days on their farm, before they were repossessed and had their way of life denatured, she says, "Once it was the family, whole and clear and there was some boundary to it. We ain't clear no more. . . . We ain't no family now."

Darwell is a wounded mother, worn down by the ravages of death and relocation. When I think of her, sometimes I think of the specific history connected to *The Grapes of Wrath*, the dust bowl, and the Depression, the stentorian beauty of the only one of Steinbeck's novels I've ever really loved. But I also generalize Darwell and her indelibly harrowed look: mothers lose their families, families lose their mothers. My own mother seemed like a balloon whose air was leaking as soon as my brother and I left home. And she just up and died soon after. I know this is reductive, and more to the point, perhaps mistaken. That's why it's called *emotional history*.

From another angle, I have always thought of myself as a mother, my son just having turned eighteen. I've conformed more closely to the stereotypes of motherhood than fatherhood in many ways: having largely had the care of a child whose emotional and medical well-being I guarded, and for whom I cooked and cleaned, on whom I lavished, as was the wont of my Eastern European background, kisses. And now that he has left, I feel bereft. My sense of family for the last almost-twenty years has been small but intense: relegated to two. And my son seems determined to break hard and fast, has decided like Huckleberry Finn, to "light out for the Territory and not look back." My own teenaged separations were slower and sloppier. I want to say, "We was the family. Kind of whole and clear." But what's the use? Jane Darwell, my mother, me . . . we lose our children and grieve. As another great screen mother surrogate, Lillian Gish in *Night of the Hunter*, says, in James Agee's prose: "The wind blows and the rains are cold, yet they [our children] abide."

* * *

I grew up going to the theater in New York, and I may have seen Elizabeth Wilson onstage more than any other actor. I saw her perform in *Plaza Suite* (1968), *The Good Woman of Setzuan* (1970), *Sticks and Bones* (1972), *Uncle Vanya* (1973), *Threepenny Opera* (1976), *Mornings at Seven* (1980) and *Ah, Wilderness* (1988), a period that ranges for me from the ages of eleven to thirty-one. I remember her as a kind of theatrical royalty of my younger years, a great and flexible actress, who happened to be just a few years older than my mother. These days she is remembered almost exclusively as the mother of Benjamin Braddock, Dustin Hoffman in *The Graduate*, though she was a memorable mother, too, in *Little Murders*, it is of these two performances I would like to speak.

Both *The Graduate* (1967), written by Buck Henry and Calder Willingham and directed by Mike Nichols, and *Little Murders* (1971), written by Jules Feiffer and directed by Alan Arkin, are satires, though *Little Murders* is an absurd, a surreal satire, while *The Graduate*'s distortions are more plausible and recognizable. In both, Elizabeth Wilson plays a mother, of

Ben, the protagonist of *The Graduate*, and of Patsy Newquist (played by Marcia Rodd) who is attempting to woo and conquer Elliott Gould in *Little Murders*. Neither role is terribly large, but both are indelible.

Elizabeth Wilson is a very attractive mother to Ben in *The Graduate*, an Oedipal conjunction to Mrs. Robinson, with whom, of course, he is having an ill-fated affair. The two women are around the same age and have similar bearings, though Wilson was a bit reedy—she seemed taller than she was. But she projects a voluptuousness in *The Graduate* that isn't quite there elsewhere, and it fits the taboo maternal implosions of the film. In one scene, at the end of the brilliant confusion of "The Sound of Silence" sequence, as Ben moves from home to hotel room with Mrs. Robinson in almost seamless editing, Wilson watches him approach their pool, and she turns as we watch her watch him. It would be easy to mistake his mother for Mrs. Robinson, their coiffed poise. But it's important to note that this is the one clear break in point of view in the entire film that I'm aware of. Nichols shoots the scene from Mrs. Braddock's (Elizabeth Wilson's) point of view, and we're left, for a brief few moments, to wonder what this mother thinks of her son, how her inner life is making sense of his. As much as the film is celebrated as incarnating a new kind of alienated subjectivity in Dustin Hoffman's Ben Braddock, I think the years have been kind to the portrayal of Ann Bancroft's Mrs. Robinson, but I'd like to further the case for the less discussed Elizabeth Wilson.

In addition to the deep poignance of the point-of-view scene, where we're left to project the questions and anxieties any parent has about a child who is growing up, confused, moving on, perhaps struggling in the process, the other scene of real engagement between mother and son (the emotionally significant interactions between Ben and others in *The Graduate* are all with women—Ben apparently has no friends, and older men—his father, Mr. Robinson, his landlord in Berkeley—are all caricatures, stereotypes of different kinds of patriarchal cluelessness, or befuddlement, rage, or paranoia).

Apparently the only template for a way forward for a young man in the film's moral economy is innocence and betrayal: Ben not yet corrupted by the world but willing to violate the norms of his parents, his parents' friends—thus, Mrs. Robinson (her first name is never given). The transition to the bathroom scene between mother and son is Wilson, Mrs. Braddock, telling Ben to "say hello to Mrs. Robinson," as she appears above him at the pool, in a hazed-out background of sun. Cut to Mrs. Braddock coming into her son's foggy bathroom as he shaves, dressed in a black negligee, lipstick. She looks great. And in this bathroom intimacy, her peignoir suggests the boudoir, and Mrs. Robinson. The concern she expresses seems entirely genuine. She says, seeming to know something of the answer in advance, "Benji, what do you do at night." It's an interesting way to phrase the question. We all know, after all, what anyone does at night. (Whenever I hear this question, I'm reminded of the 1939 film, with a screenplay by F. Scott Fitzgerald, *Everything Happens at Night.*) She presses the obvious: "Do you meet someone?" We know that for Ben to give an honest answer—sleeping with a woman your age, your supposed old friend—is impossible. He says, instead, "Nothing. I drive around." Frustrated, and unwilling to have what is for her an inauthentic conversation (ironically, in this scene the tables are turned on Ben, so much of this film is about communication, miscommunication) Wilson turns and walks away, as Ben, as Dustin Hoffman, says, "Wait. Will you wait a minute?" transitioning into the bedroom with Mrs. Robinson as he says, "Mrs. Robinson, will you wait a minute," wondering if they can possibly communicate a little before sex. But the point is made clearly: the doubling of line to mother and lover tells us that there is a confusion between mother and lover, lest there had been any doubt.

My own house, growing up in Brooklyn, was so very small, and my bond with my mother was too wildly close. I ended wanting to run so far away from her that in an implosion of focused necessity, I stole money from her for my first sexual relationship—with a middle-aged prostitute in an office building near Times Square (she was reasonably nice). No, I wasn't the college grad of *The Graduate*, though; I was fourteen. Hello, darkness my old friend?

Wilson has one more scene in *The Graduate* before she disappears, and it's really closer to the wild satiric tone of *Little Murders* than the subtlety of her limited but crucial scenes in Mike Nichols' film. Dustin Hoffman's Ben tells his father and his father tells his mother that he is going to marry Elaine Robinson, Mrs. Robinson's daughter. Mrs. Braddock screams—it's really something of a shriek, the kind you'd let out if you just accidentally cut your finger off. It's very funny—a moment of apparent parental exultation being rendered as horror, Buck Henry cartoony—more along the tone of the "Plastics" moment, and the scuba outfit at the bottom of the pool than some of the more genuinely subtle moments of the film, like the entirely devastating shot of Anne Bancroft's Mrs. Robinson, unglamorized and reduced, tracked at the end of the hallway, the real measure of her age perhaps about to descend on her, saying goodbye to Benjamin Braddock.

In the version of *The Graduate* I carry around, Elizabeth Wilson's glamorous Mrs. Braddock is indissolubly linked with Mrs. Robinson; a repressed and sexualized mother-son scenario that's much safer than my own was and is, and because scripted, plays out within certain well-defined boundaries on the screen, and even in my wayward memory.

In *Little Murders*, Wilson is like many of the mothers I grew up with: she does her best to avoid the anger and irrationality of her husband (who, played by Vincent Gardenia, goes into a fury whenever anyone calls him by his proper first name, Carol, because he considers it feminizing, and therefore castrating), and the neurosis of her barely repressed gay son. Her motives may seem similar to Ma Joad's—wanting to keep the family together—but as the mother of Patsy (Marcia Rodd), she plays as a bizarre parody of obliviousness. I actually have some tenderness for this weird distension of unreality, this surreal version of normalcy in the midst of chaos. It actually does remind me, in a hyperbolized way, of scenes of my childhood: the cities on fire in the '60s, the war on the evening news with body counts rising and American atrocities seeming to pop up like ghastly weeds in a garden we thought we had sterilized from the worst intrusions by having fought World War II. In some ways, Jean Stapleton's Edith Bunker was a toned-down version of this archetype.

My father, who was a reasonably liberal, anti-war, pro-labor, pro–capital punishment, casually racist, anti-Republican bundle of contradictions (at least to me), and I would scream at each other in disbelief at the other's idiocy. He thought, I'm sure, with good reason, that I was a Utopian, softhearted dreamer who had had things too easy and couldn't understand the realities of the world as they really were, which, to him, were forged in tenements, war, and years of hard work starting from the earliest age.

In the midst of all of this, my mother would—not unlike Elizabeth Wilson in *Little Murders*, or my friends' mothers, like Edith Bunker or the Virgin Mary—try to intercede, calm things down, serve meatloaf and the occasional piety or calming cliché. "So much tension. Rush, rush, rush. My mother taught me to take dainty little steps," Wilson says in the middle of one stormy episode between father, daughter, and son. Jules Feiffer, at his best in *Little Murders*, where each scene is like an animated version of his brilliant cartoons that I grew up reading in the *Village Voice*, manages to push the characters further, to somewhere between Pirandello, Chekhov, and *I Love Lucy*. And Elizabeth Wilson, having played *Vanya* on Broadway is more than up to the challenge of delivering deadpan absurd dialogue. She says to Albert (Elliott Gould), her future son-in-law, "You're a photographer, Albert, so I thought you'd be interested in seeing these pictures of Patsy's dead brother Steve. He pitched three no hitters." She's not exactly Mrs. Miniver, and that's the point: Greer Garson wasn't a character actor, and not only couldn't have pulled off the straightforward derangement implicit in these lines, but probably wouldn't have wanted to; they would have damaged her image. Elizabeth Wilson had the range, from Brecht to Albee to Wilde, to modulate this mother of the cusp of the '70s from sympathetic to almost mad. Near the end of *Little Murders*, after her daughter's murder, and her household's quick descent into mayhem, Wilson has a compact monologue that blends an idyllic nostalgia and the mundane, one leading into the other without transition, which echoes her own wavering sanity: "There were so many flowers in those days. We'd pick every last one and bring them back to the city. No one does the cleaning around here except me."

Little Murders is a film constructed of character performances: Gould, Gardenia, along with set pieces by Lou Jacobi, Alan Arkin, and an especially brilliant turn by Donald Sutherland. It was a time when cities and families didn't seem to make much sense anymore as organizing principles: they were scary, estranging, sometimes astonishingly violent in ways we never thought home should or could be. But then, frequently, in the midst of all that, came mother. "Hold me Mom, in your long arms," Laurie Anderson sings, chillingly on "O Superman." "In your electronic arms": so much for succor.

When the trauma of Patsy's arbitrary murder sends the family into full-scale psychosis, her son, son-in-law, and husband start indiscriminately shooting people out the window. Patsy's mother sits them down for a nice family dinner. She says, "Oh, you don't know how good it is to hear my family laughing again. You know, for a while there, I was really worried." This catharsis that restores the meatloaf, that puts everyone back at the table talking, is a catharsis that makes gruesome sense. Elizabeth Wilson is like Donna Reed after a lobotomy. It's chilling, and funny, and especially discomfiting: strangely familiar.

* * *

Finally, just a few words about all those Hitchcock mothers, missing and present. "Mother's here," Barbara Bel Geddes says to the mute James Stewart (Scottie) in *Vertigo* (1958), after he's been traumatized by the apparent death of Kim Novak, whom he thinks is Madeleine Elster. It's a wonderfully creepy moment, the spurned lover ministering as mother.

Perhaps no other Hitchcock mother can be as interesting to me as Jesse Royce Landis, whom I've written of elsewhere— mother to Cary Grant (she was seven years older) in *North by Northwest*, and to Grace Kelly in *To Catch a Thief*, so the prospective mother-in-law to Cary Grant (she was still seven years older). No mother-in-law has ever been more seductive, and no mother has ever been more casually dismissive of her son in films that I can think of.

It isn't that Hitchcock couldn't do a turn on more conventional motherhood: Esther Minciotti's supportive and somewhat stereotypical Italian mother to Henry Fonda in *The Wrong Man*, or Doris Day—well, her "Que Sera" performance in *The Man Who Knew Too Much* redux I. (I've always thought what Doris Day could have been as an actress is there if you listen to her recordings, watch some earlier performances, like *Love Me or Leave Me* with James Cagney.) Here I have to interrupt to do a partial correction: the iconic scene in *The Man Who Knew Too Much* in which Doris Day's voice leads to her son, and his safety from kidnappers, is a piece of bravura kitsch that does always hook me, but it's not because of Day's performance, not at all; it's the *idea* of the scene, along with the catchiness of the song that makes the experience emotionally irresistible: a mother's voice (some version of Eurydice?) can lead to safety, can lead away from death. My mother used to sing it sometimes in her own sweet soprano.

Hitchcock's own mother, Emma Jane Hitchcock, had been dead for almost fifteen years when he made *The Man Who Knew Too Much*. Nevertheless he wanted to embody the power of a mother's voice as life affirming, as life saving. Can one hear it through corridors, from floor to floor, after fifteen years, after thirty?

I struggle to remember my own mother's voice these days. I remember the fact of an accent. An occasional hint of timbre and tone. It's a ghostly passing of aural memory. But were the actual voice to break into song somewhere in this hemisphere, I'm sure the ropes binding my hands would snap and I'd run toward it with all the dispatch I've got left in my still nimble but, let's face it, aging legs. No, they'd never get me.

* * *

All of these actresses have filled my thoughts of motherhood over the decades. I've been fixing that hole for about forty years, partially by superimposition, and partially by a kind of imitation: myself as mother. Yes, I know, *Psycho* comes to mind: "I wouldn't hurt a fly." One of most outlandish portrayals of a mother in film. Such a devoted son. I can't say much for his taste in clothes or decor, but he clearly loved his mother to death.

MY FAMILY ROMANCE

EDWARD EVERETT HORTON AND JESSIE ROYCE LANDIS

One of my first memories of the movies is somewhat incestu-
ous. I remember walking into my parents' bedroom in our row
house in Brooklyn, the black-and-white TV screen throwing
light from a corner. My parents were supine, each on his or
her side of their trundle bed. They were murmuring, talking
in that affectless tone of remarking that people use when the
tube is on and they're actually watching it in a kind of listless
way while also paying nominal attention to each other. Their
heads were toward the door, and they couldn't see me come in.
I wanted to get closer to them, to hear what connubial words
were being exchanged in the bluish TV-screen light. A movie
was showing, something from the '40s or '30s, it seemed, a
mansion, men in evening dress, women in dressy dresses. I
moved closer and heard my father's voice more clearly; he was
saying things like Joseph Schildkraut, S. Z. Sakall, Marjorie
Main, James Gleason, Patsy Kelly, Elisha Cook, Edward Everett
Horton. He was naming the characters who swirled around

19. Edward Everett Horton. James Hargis
Connelly, Chicago / Wikimedia Commons.

20. Jessie Royce Landis. United States
Steel / Wikimedia Commons.

the margins, never far from the lead actors but sometimes moved off-screen after one brief line, one double take, a short verbal effusion, or a bit of physical business. Whatever it was they did, it was something my parents noticed.

I looked at my parents, looked at the screen, back and forth; if I could magically transport back and see myself watching the scene, I'm sure I'd look like a child detective standing in the semi-dark, trying to solve a mystery. How could they know the names of such unimportant players? *Why* would they? Sometimes little grunts and groans of delight seemed to urge out of them at the mention of a particular name, like the noises I would learn to make at an amuse-bouche. I tiptoed out, and wondered how these people had spent their lives, and why—also, they didn't have a door that locked.

Little did I know that I would find myself, decades later, engaged in a similar supine pursuit, although the room is larger, as is the TV, and in color, the mattress singularly firm and large and hypoallergenic, no one stepping up stealthily while I watch to hear me murmuring to myself, and miles from Brooklyn before I sleep.

Ward Bond, Beulah Bondi, Arthur Treacher, Binnie Barnes. Character actors all. Their names almost feel like musty passwords of a secret society. And a related category to character actors: the second leads, who may or may not be character actors; some of them were hacks who were just narrative place cards, but others were creatures of the bad break who studio heads didn't think had enough wattage, or whose lead light had faded for whatever reason. One of my favorites was Lew Ayres, who started a star, but then was wrecked when he declared as a CO in World War II. He ended multi-medaled as a combat medic and was nominated for an Oscar for Johnny

Belinda, but his career never fully recovered. I've always loved those second leads who stuck around long enough to take, or fall into, the lead, even if, or perhaps especially when, these vocational promotions were never quite convincing: Don Ameche, Eddie Bracken, Jack Carson. Of course, there is the occasional actor or actress who blurs the line: Van Johnson (I may be the only remaining Van Johnson fan under a certain age—his portrait of grief in *The Last Time I Saw Paris* almost unwatchably good, his line readings spoken with a kind of tartness that would get Tom Cruise slapped; beyond that, he's always good), or Gloria Grahame, who won an Oscar, had a long career with name sometimes above the title, but never transcended a certain sultriness, other than perhaps in *In a Lonely Place*, a superbly modern and affecting performance, created under difficult circumstances (directed by Nicholas Ray, from whom she was separating), which is why she is in my pantheon of Hollywood sirens.

The character actor who becomes and stays a star is epitomized by Judy Holliday, who, in my fantasy life, I have escaped with many times to Tahiti or the Bronx. She is the only actress I know who can completely pull off a goofy sexuality without undermining either quality. On top of it, she adds a devastating vulnerability. Holliday pulled off a kind character actress coup de théâtre, winning the Academy Award for *Born Yesterday,* in 1950, over Bette Davis and Anne Baxter in *All About Eve* and Gloria Swanson in *Sunset Boulevard.*

Since I can't run away with Judy Holliday, I may as well fantastically marry off my two all-time favorite character actors, my cinematic parents, who I hope have a sexy reaction formation: Edward Everett Horton and Jessie Royce Landis. But before we reach the nuptials, or the deepest part of my dreamwork, lest anyone object, perhaps I should explain why these two are, in my book, heroic, and why I hope they have a strange and delightful lifetime together in my mind.

They are heroic because I do not have much of an appreciation of conventional heroism. Hold that: I should say, instead, that it doesn't interest me terribly. Rather than noble and inspiring acts, I am much more drawn to interesting and endearing people. Understandably, perhaps, the world lauds character as a signal virtue, but I tend to laud characters who are heroic to me in the way they expand the human franchise of individuality, even peculiarity, or embody qualities I find underrepresented or unique in combination. That is my idea of heroism, the bravery of expanding typologies of character, and as Eric Idle of Monty Python says, when asked what it is: it is mine. It is never easy to be different, lest you think I'm being glib.

My family romance will be united by a unique blend of sophistication and benign xenophobia, which is to say my fantasy parents will be well dressed but unable to speak French. They are savvy Americans in their way, Horton and Landis, these bewildered nouveaux riche, when ordering champagne. They have a general aversion to foreign culture, especially French, which they submit to out of a clear enough sense that it's the thing to do—to do business. For example: managing the great Petrov (Fred Astaire) in *Shall We Dance?* in Horton's case; or to show the world that one's daughter is "finished," as is the case with Landis in *To Catch a Thief*. You have to put aside your prejudices when you're an American in Nice. In the former case, in Paris, Horton asks, "Ou est Petrov?" with the consternation of a man for whom language generally is a minefield and a foreign language a minefield that one must crawl across knowing that an explosion is inevitable nonetheless. In the latter, Jesse Royce Landis, in *To Catch a Thief*, at a surreally elaborate costume party on the Riviera, drops her sense of masquerade to ask a bartender, "Avez-vous bourbon?"—the third word inflected with the pique of a woman who is so comfortable being herself but so tired of being abroad that any pretense is a chore requiring a foolproof and homegrown tonic.

They move in heady circles, these two, and their clothes are tailored and expensive, but they are resolutely unpretentious. My mother's fit better than my father's, and yet I don't want to really think about why that is.

* * *

My own father was rather ego strong, overbearing, so I sometimes think it would be lovely to have a witty, slightly befuddled, somewhat impotent father who could also do world-class double takes. He would, of course, be impotent in the right way: a de-testosteroned personality, if not completely lacking bite, gentle, neither overengaged nor underinvolved, with three-piece tweed suits that looked pretty natty despite the fact that his body was a bit hippy.

Their voices: his (Horton's) has a squeak that comes and goes, a bit of patrician New York, with a steady waver, and an unexpectedly musical effect, up and down the scales, calibrated to enter a wisecrack or a surreally self-effacing moment at a strangely pleasing tenor pitch; her voice is mezzo, the accent hints at a lower class that has moved up, rounded out, a Boston Brahmin via Dubuque, and when she speaks you feel her sense of balanced certainty, and that this certainty is as qualified as anything else, which is to say *rather*. You know she's been around: perhaps from the Orpheum Circuit to Famous-Players-Lasky to disappointing contracts at Warner's or RKO.

He proves it is possible to be heroically flustered, as he indulges in epically neurotic concern for details that diverge from the expected; sometimes his own strange practices—the way he lives—follows a grammar of logic that he thinks is completely normal, but no one seems to understand. When he tries to explain, it's like he's explicating the mores of a country with one inhabitant.

She shows a heroically mature feminine sexuality, matched with a mocking wit. You can see in the twinkle of her eyes when she looks at Cary Grant, either as son or as her daughter's lover, that she likes handsome men, even if she thinks they're ridiculous.

His tie is askew, and his shoes come untied. "Oh, dear," he might say. "First Calvin Coolidge, now this." Her dress is satin, a strap hangs off one fifty-five-year-old shoulder. If she caught you looking, she might say, "It's a fallen world, after all," and give you a complex half smile.

Her eyes widen suggestively. His narrow perplexedly.

My heroic father does not wander like Odysseus, but he is very amusing while looking for his socks. My heroic mother does not sacrifice interminably, or wait by the window like Penelope, but she looks smashing in a long silk robe, with matching slippers that she mocks.

He's slightly bent but looks good in a tux that he claims is uncomfortable, or a three-piece tweed that almost makes you want to wear a vest. His fedora is at an angle, and damn if he doesn't look almost handsome, despite a complex nose that vies with his brim. And he moves with fluidity, which his awkward body would never suggest.

In *To Catch a Thief*, the Cat, Cary Grant, is under quiet threat of seduction by Grace Kelly, centuries younger than him, whom he initially resists—an absurd idea but perhaps the only possible response to such cool perfection. That, or prostration. The famous kiss outside her hotel room, the two having just met: she takes him head in hands and plants one on him, and he looks like the Cat who swallowed a canary. It's the same look of sexual luck that Grant also flashes on the train to Eva Marie Saint in *North by Northwest*, when she says that she never makes love before eating. But it is Grace Kelley's mother in the film, Jessie Royce Landis's seduction of the Cat *for* her daughter that I'm . . . more seduced by, her casual air of what's wrong with you for not making love to my beautiful daughter? And while seducing the Cat as a suitor for her daughter, with the indefatigable air of someone who recognizes that the sexual arts have entered a decadent and altogether clumsy age, Landis flirts beautifully with Cary Grant herself, culminating in the moment that will always be for me the Ur-look of seduction: the Cat is searching Landis's hotel room for signs of the copy Cat he is tracking, the jewel thief who is framing him. He turns to Jessie Royce Landis and says, "You must sleep soundly." She says, "I do," a matrimonial avowal, but with the flicker of a smirk and the slow closing of eyes saying so much more. Quite frankly, what they silently say is the word "fuck" in every possible permutation. It isn't quite an invitation, although *it* verges. It's much deeper than a boast but too confident for a come-on. It's an unflinching assertion of sexual prowess, made to a potential son-in-law, who it just so happens is almost exactly her age. If Landis is a heroine of sexual self-knowledge and droll self-mockery, considering the situation, she would almost have to be.

* * *

To interrupt a laugh with a jolt of self-knowledge usually means you've learned the joke's on you. One turns *isn't that amusing* into *aren't I a fool*. But to do so with a sense of comic dignity, to signal indignity with dignity, is the quality that holy fools possess. They can change laughs in midstream. Horton's version of this, though, isn't sentimental; it's an urban version, and the ultimate message is that sophistication is an occasionally desirable quality of limited value. "Elia, thou art sophisticated," Charles Lamb says to himself in a bemused moment of recognition in the essay "New Year's Eve." He was not wearing a tuxedo. In Edward Everett Horton's case, we think, in gratitude, *thou can never be really sophisticated*, if we understand the use of sophistication to mean elegant, refined, well mannered.

His head strides into a room ahead of his body, the walking stick he carries looking more like a tail than an accoutrement.

She moves languorously and knowingly in clothes that few can afford and few care less about.

For Edward Everett Horton, the art of indignation usually involves a midair correction. He agrees, wholeheartedly, until he realizes that he disagrees completely. In *Shall We Dance?*, a classic example of how the simplest series of line deliveries can be riotously original, especially when spoken with a sincerity that belies any attempt to be casually pusillanimous, Horton says, in response to a question meant to elicit his guilt: "Yes. That is, not exactly. No." These lines sum up the film's ambiguities, the high and low culture, ballet and tap dancing, in a sharp distillation of comic confusion. Even though Horton wants his friend and client, the great Petrov (Fred Astaire), to continue with the art of the ballet, he makes us understand that no one as confused as he could represent a pure cultural ideology. His confusion liberates Fred Astaire to do exactly what he wants and sets in motion my hyperextended analysis of this piece of popular culture. Yes? Not exactly? No?

* * *

The scene of laughter and forgetting, in the elevator, in *North by Northwest*: Cary Grant cannot convince his mother—Jesse Royce Landis doing a more tart reprise of her role in *To Catch a Thief*—that he is in danger. Crowded into the hotel elevator with the men who want to kill Roger O. Thornhill, her son, Landis looks at the men and asks if they are trying to kill him. Her delivery of the line is the engine of the scene: very American in its directness, but with more than a hint of absurdity. She starts laughing, as does every other woman on the elevator. The laughter goes from a slightly giddy disbelief to a kind of hysteria, the killers heartily joining in. Landis throws her head back and you can see for an instant her distant background in silent film. Everyone is laughing but her son, Cary Grant. This is the stuff of nightmares, specifically Freudian ones. How else, after all, could one respond to a son's public avowal that two men huddled close in a small room plunging downward are cold killers? It sounds like a joke, so it must be one. Landis-Mother's infectious laughter is castrating; it's one of our worst fears, a nightmare vision really, to be publicly humiliated by our mothers—and here Hitchcock's mother fixation burns out of the screen as brightly as in *Psycho*—but Landis ultimately creates the dramaturgical extravagance of Grant's exit, his escape. Her laughter is the indulgence of unalloyed skepticism, yes, extended by the hilarity in her eyes, their combination of innocence and experience—a particularly American marriage of naivete and knowingness. But this move lets him live. Lest a mother's disbelief in her son's turmoil, his potentially fatal mistaken identity, be perceived as unheroic, it is important to note that her skepticism is a function of his own character flaw, his failure to invest authentically in anything. What does the *O.* in his middle name stand for, he's asked—"Nothing." And despite her witheringly witty responses to the quagmire of confusion and danger he has gotten himself into, she can be cajoled into helping him, all along acting as though life were quite ridiculous, and her son absurd, and these particulars were merely an extension of life's normally wacky vicissitudes. Landis is a heroine of the oedipally surreal. She is the perfect Hitchcock mother.

And surreal will describe her wedding to Edward Everett Horton (the ceremony performed, perhaps, by Jacques Tati? He's French, but never speaks). It's true that Edward Everett Horton was gay, part of the long history of closeted Hollywood, but since this is a family romance, my fractured fairy tale, there's no reason I can't arrange a lavender marriage. They'll both take lovers but remain devoted. I can hardly wait to see Landis's face, or perhaps to hear her laugh. Horton will murmur, "Oh, dear," and she will look at him with muted, bemused astonishment, not quite sure of how she got there, not quite sure of why I'm doing this to her, but with a sense of the weirdness of fate. She'll acknowledge she did *something* to put her in this predicament, perhaps being too interesting (that almost never seems to work), or she might just find the whole thing terribly amusing. Horton will announce himself as ready as he'll ever be. I know that he can handle a strong woman, since his marriage with Susan (played by Ruth Donnelly) in *Holiday* is one of the great screen relationships, perhaps my favorite of all. I do feel a bit like a cinematic home-wrecker interjecting this, but this couple has inspired me for decades, much as it inspires Cary Grant and Katharine Hepburn in the 1938 film (the film was first made in 1930, with Horton playing the same role). What makes this marriage between Professor Nick and Susan Potter magical is what also makes Grant and Hepburn so good together: a sense of play suggesting a profound knowledge of one's partner. It sounds simple until you realize that cosmic chemistry sets are almost never on sale. This is Horton's best role because he gets to play to his intelligence as a professor, while also acting ridiculous, as unlikely as that combination may seem, as opposed to his delightful but more one-dimensional roles in many other films.

Wit and affection are the household gods here, and Horton invokes them with the élan of a seasoned practitioner. I would be remiss if I didn't mention the extraordinary performance of Jean Dixon, playing an older proto-feminist role model to Katherine Hepburn, and with sympathy and comic timing that matches Edward Everett Horton, she makes them believable as a couple. She was a favorite of George S. Kaufmann, and based on her timing, one can understand why, though her film career never really took off. Grant and Hepburn, Dixon and Everett Horton, and marvelous Lew Ayres as a sad young drunk, along with James Barrie's play, and Donald Ogden Stewart's script of the same, and George Cukor's usual finesse with actors, make a usually graceful though sometimes heavy-handed attack on class pretensions; no actor displays this more amusingly than Edward Everett Horton losing his shoe in a galosh to an over-attentive butler at the entrance to a stately Fifth Avenue mansion and trying obsequiously, and then determinedly, to retrieve it as he limps around a grand foyer that impresses him as impressively unfamiliar. "It seems to have been a residence of some kind at one point," he says drolly to his wife. She looks at him with killer deadpan, a non-acknowledgment that is the perfect familiar acknowledgment between long-together couples.

It is in *Holiday* that Horton is most heroic, in my terms, because he is an unusual man who insists on being himself, and his performance here, which was I'm sure the first of his I ever saw, has colored every subsequent performance I've seen. It is heroic because it is honorable and eccentric. He is amusingly, dedicatedly himself, devoted to those he loves, and free of institutional investment. Note some wishful thinking on my part? What are heroes for? After all, I find the idea of running into burning buildings a miracle of adrenalized fear-repression and have been unimpressed with most "great deeds" since I was eleven, finding in most a self-aggrandizing quality that makes me queasy.

Edward Everett Horton and Jesse Royce Landis will be quite happy together. I believe: they'll talk about their sex lives after I've gone to bed, over a martini or two, fueled by good humor, and they won't take any guff from anyone who pretends to more than their own very American, slightly kooky, occasionally sharp-tongued vision of character. I'm proud of my parents, and if this isn't heroism pour me an epic and pass the ammunition, but keep the lights down low so we can still see the screen: my father in black and white, my mother in color.

21. Martin Balsam. Wikimedia Commons.

22. Leo Lazar. Courtesy of the author.

MARTIN BALSAM

THE BEST POSSIBLE ARNOLD BURNS

He was born in 1919 to an Eastern European Jewish family in New York—his parents, immigrants, Yiddish speaking—and graduated from DeWitt Clinton High School in the Bronx. He was in the military in World War II and served in the Third Theater, the Pacific-Asian Theater, which encompassed the war in the Pacific, Japan, the Philippines, and so on, but also Australia and India for support services. He rose to the rank of sergeant. After the war, demobbed, he returned to New York. He longed to hear his parents' Yiddish again.

There are probably a few dozen men who fit this description, but two of them are my father and the character actor Martin Balsam, who appeared in dozens of films and won an Academy Award in 1965 for *A Thousand Clowns*. They knew each other well, though I'm not sure if they knew each other in high school. They did not serve together in the war, but I remember my father talking about "Marty" from a reasonably early age. My father, who owned a thriving travel agency in midtown Manhattan (Comet Travel Service—I came up with the name when I was five, because comets are fast) that served the garment industry, had many "celebrity" clients over the years: Perry Como, Shirley Bassey, Danny Kaye. It was New York, and my father, over the years, through his charm and ability to hustle, through sheer indomitable will, established himself as a person in the travel business who could "get the tough ticket," the difficult reservation, which was useful to . . . almost everyone, an eminently tradeable skill. And reputation, as we know, becomes tradeable itself; so once my father had established that reputation it built on itself, and he became in certain circles a, shall we say, figure of some repute (I feel like I should be Keenan Wynn saying this in a pin-striped suit, though my father was no Ed Wynn), in other words, a character.

To add to this, my father, in the pursuit of airline tickets, hotel reservations, whatever arrangements he needed to make for his clients (and then, whatever arrangements he needed to make for his sons' insatiable need for concert tickets and the family's desire for tickets to Broadway shows) turned himself, at some point, plastic and fungible, an actor who could get what he needed for himself and others. I've written elsewhere about my child's-eye version of this, my father's "John Waterman" phone in his office first on West Thirty-Seventh Street, and then for many years on West Thirty-Third Street, across from Madison Square Garden. The John Waterman phone was a phone in my father's office that we were instructed never to pick up, that my father would use to play any character he needed to be to get what he wanted, usually for a client. If a hotel was booked up, or a flight, my father would be governmental, perhaps the mayor's deputy—people didn't, couldn't, check things as much fifty years ago—or some other flight of fancy he had: a famous Australian thespian, the visiting mayor of Bismarck, North Dakota. My father loved to do accents. That was part of his character actors' shtick.

Martin Balsam, the character actor, had a bland, almost generic American accent. It makes sense that he was the original voice of the HAL-9000 computer in *2001: A Space Odyssey*. I can just hear his voice saying, "Dave," and it's too bad that Kubrick replaced it (sounded too American to him) because I would have forever loved that connection: Balsam, friend of my father from the Bronx, and, through Kubrick, my name spoken to freaked-out Keir Dullea. But one of the hallmarks of Balsam's most interesting career as a character actor is the way he falls between the two classic modes of great character actors: quirky personalities imprinted on most roles no matter how different, or the disappearing of the individual into a distinctly different character each time. He was neither, or perhaps a kind of strange combination of the two: he brought a kind of *indistinct character* to each role that seemed vaguely familiar but was like a theme with variations.

My father used to refer to him as "Marty," and after Marty moved from New York to California, he would call my father, once a week, or so, and they would speak Yiddish to each other. (Now I'm hearing the HAL-9000 voice say my name with a Yiddish-inflected accent.) When he needed a ticket, his assistant would call. I never met him or talked to him, unlike the many other actors who were clients of my father that I got the opportunity to drool over in my childhood. And that's it, that's about all I know of the connection between these two sergeants, these characters, other than a story my brother reminded me of, which I'd forgotten. After doing so many films of such high quality: *Psycho* (still probably his best-known role, though small, as the detective Arbogast, who dies at the hand of Anthony Perkins's "mother" in a famous tracking shot down the stairs), *On the Waterfront*, *Twelve Angry Men*, *Breakfast at Tiffany's*, *Cape Fear*, *Seven Days in May*, *Catch-22*, *Little Big Man*, Balsam, who also had an extensive TV resume, was offered bags of money to co-star with Carroll O'Connor in *Archie's Place*, the spin-off continuation of *All in the Family*, starring Carroll O'Connor. After a year, apparently, he was bored with it and asked my father if he thought he should stay. My father, predictably, told him he would be an idiot to walk about from so much dough.

My father had many virtues, but a reasonable perspective on the value of money was not one of them. The house I grew up in (for some reason I have an unseasonal nostalgia for that phrase, "the house I grew up in," with its dangling preposition suggesting so many possibilities: *in* thrall with movies, *in* constant anxiety about what kind of bizarre creature I was, *in* a surfeit of melancholy about whether I was loved or would be, and so on, not to mention how *house* functions like a clinging vine of nostalgia, extending to so many associations that our enclosures represent, psychologically, emotionally, somatically) was to some extent governed by sayings, a combination of clichés and epigrams pulled from familial experience. One that my father repeated often was, "It all come down to money." Freethinking anti-capitalist teenager that I was, I hated it. I recently suggested, ruefully, to my brother as we contemplated the inscription on my father's headstone that we write, "It all comes down to money." He seemed amused. If you have older siblings, you understand how much of the psychic energy of your lives comes from the discipline of trying to amuse them.

In any case, Martin Balsam, after a long career of roles, walked away from one that was particularly bland.

None of this would matter if I weren't interested in Balsam in some way, if I didn't find something interesting or essential about some of his performances; the quality or qualities I've always been most intrigued by are most represented by his award-winning role in *A Thousand Clowns*, where he plays the brother of protagonist Murray Burns (Jason Robards), Arnold Burns.

A Thousand Clowns is really a dated film in many ways, with its vague and sentimental ideology of pre-1960s dropout bliss combined with a kind of curdled New York cynicism. It's at times delightful and at times somewhat distasteful. As is frequently, if not inevitably true of great character actor performances, Balsam has many good and one great scene. He plays the "straight" foil to his unconventional brother, Murray (Jason Robards); Arnold is the manager to his writer brother, the creative, quirky, and unpredictable sibling who, rejecting the compromises of commercial TV, has dropped out. I have to digress briefly, before talking about Balsam's "big scene," to mention the character performance of Gene Saks in *A Thousand Clowns*. Saks, who went on to an astonishing seven Tony nominations, winning three for directing, here plays a children's TV host who is desperately unfunny and bleeds neurosis. It's a strange and very funny performance, one of the great demonstrations of tonal inversion—the comedy of being unfunny (like the tragedy of alexithymia, the inability to experience emotion). Saks, as Leo, who plays Chuckles the Chipmunk on TV, berates Barry Gordon's Nick (Murray and Arnold's nephew) for telling him how sad and unfunny he is, as though the rudeness of the boy's honesty were some kind of elixir that could cancel out the essence of its truth. It's a scene worthy of Beckett, really, thanks to Saks.

Martin Balsam's Arnold has been trying to persuade Murray, his brother, to take any job, including writing for sad Leo again, just to have some income so he can show he's fit to keep custody of his nephew. In other words, he pitches the virtues of compromise and sacrifice. Very "square." In one scene he breaks down laughing, against his will, at Murray's description of having left one potential employer flatfooted. This is 1965 (on film—Herb Gardner's play *A Thousand Clowns* debuted on Broadway in 1962) and Jason Robards's Murray is a prototypical, and early, '60s free spirit. "I would have loved to have seen that," Arnold says. "It must have been great. I wish to God I didn't enjoy you so much." But the central scene is later the same day, after Murray has walked out of Murray's office and blown the interview with Chuckles that Arnold, that Balsam, has worked so hard to salvage so that Murray could once again write for the sad clown. Balsam, eager to confront Jason Robards's Murray, seeks him out and confronts him.

"You said I insulted you," Robards says, trying to get a rise out of his too tolerant brother. "Please, please have an argument with me." But Arnold is eternally mollifying and wants Murray to try again. Arnold responds with a long monologue defending his resistance to conformity. As he walks away, Balsam shouts his name—it's really an ejaculation—and says, "Ooh, I scared myself." What follows is probably the best minute of Balsam's career and the reason he won the Academy Award. Balsam delivers Herb Gardner's moving and unconvincing defense of mediocrity. He says,

I have a wife and I have children, and business as they say is business. I'm not an exceptional man, so it's possible for me to stay with things the way they are. I'm lucky. I'm gifted; I have a talent for surrender. And I'm at peace. But you, you're cursed. And I like you, Murray. It makes me sad. You don't have the gift, and I can see the torture of it. All I can do is worry for you, but I will not worry for myself. You can't convince me that I'm one of the bad guys. I get up. I go. I lie a little. I peddle a little. I watch the rules. I talk the talk. We fellows have those offices high up there so we can catch the wind and go with it however it blows. But—and I'm not going to apologize for it—I take pride: I am the best possible Arnold Burns.

The scene is on YouTube, so I urge you to watch it; it's riveting and captures Martin Balsam's great ability to be a distinct, even a perfect everyman, to explore the boundary between "normalcy" and idiosyncrasy. Balsam had a round face, a receding hairline. He looked like the eternal model for Willy Loman, or your accountant. That actually meant he could play an endless variety of middle-aged roles, frequently roles in which the character is in some ways blocked, defeated, stymied. His look was the opposite of heroic, though it wasn't, as he says in his *Thousand Clowns* speech, the stuff of intense antagonists. He could be memorably rueful, or slightly pathetic at his best. As Mr. Longman/Mr. Green in *The Taking of Pelham 1-2-3*, Balsam is a nervous, down on his luck motorman, and, ironically, the one hijacker to escape. We aren't sure who to root for at the end—Matthau the cop, or the guy (Balsam) in his robe with a cold.

Usually he played highly articulate roles. Like my father, and many other New York ethnic borough kids, Balsam clearly valued speech: think of Frank Sinatra's brilliant, innovative lyrical articulation in the '50s. I remember my own efforts to rid myself of my Brooklyn accent in my midteens, when even other kids with Brooklyn accents commented on how pronounced mine was. Quite a feat! But of course not every character actor flattens out their accent; many in fact trade on the uniqueness of it: Sheldon Leonard, Thelma Ritter.

Balsam had studied at the Dramatic Workshop at New School with Erwin Piscator, and right after the war Elia Kazan asked him to join the new Actors' Studio. How heady it must have been for a young Jewish actor, postwar, to have been an innkeeper in *The Living Christ Series*, an early TV series about the life of Jesus, or to be cast as Gillette, the investigator in Kazan's *On the Waterfront*. In 1957 he was one of the jurors in *Twelve Angry Men*, though in truth, Balsam's role as foreman, somewhat halting, pretty reasonably, pretty *reasonable*, isn't the first that comes to mind. That is emblematic for Martin Balsam: always good, serving character, not usually the first thing that pops into memory when you try to think of performances that turned your head.

Of course, there's Arbogast. In *Psycho*, Balsam as the detective hired to pursue the disappearance of Janet Leigh has one of the most famous death scenes in cinema. When I speak to people about actors, about character actors, quite frankly, most people don't know Balsam—they ask what he was in, and after the first few films I mention, a vague film of memory seems to form that solidifies, perhaps, with Arbogast—which takes me aback, considering the number of films he had supporting roles in, more recently than many character actors who seem to have stayed more durably in memory. It's because, I think, his performances were so un-quirky, quite different from undistinguished. But Arbogast will always be something of a calling card.

If you remember, Arbogast, thinking he must talk to Anthony Perkins's mother, has gone to the Bates house and is walking up the stairs, hoping to meet Mother. Bernard Hermann's music is cueing us the whole way, through his strained strings, that this is not a good situation. The subjective point of view jumps: from Arbogast's to the objective view, a boom shot from the top of the stairs, of him climbing. An objective view of a door opening increasing our sense of dread; suddenly the door flies open, at which point Hitchcock switches radically, briefly, to an overhead shot of Perkins's mother running out of the room and stabbing Arbogast. The camera then focuses on Arbogast-Balsam's face, bloodied with cuts, eyes wide open, mouth open, stunned arms waving like a bird, flailing and falling backward down the stairs in a tracking shot, as Bernard Hermann's famous *Psycho* strings accompany Arbogast's downfall. After he lands at the bottom, the knife is lifted high for an isolated shot, held for just an instant, then plunged, and we hear his muffled scream. And the scene ends. It's one of the most shocking and memorable deaths in cinema.

And I think it's so memorable because, in a sense, Balsam, to his credit, both is and isn't. He isn't the protagonist, he isn't good looking or young and promising. He's a middle-aged guy doing his job, and he's very much in the wrong place—this death both complements and contrasts with Janet Leigh's. She's the beautiful woman symbolically being punished for her guilt. Arbogast's death is everyman meeting a kind of existential chaos. His physiognomy, his unthreatening, reasonable countenance, makes the violence done to him all the more horrific. And Balsam's open-mouthed, fish-like terror has the vérité of someone caught in a real nightmare.

* * *

My father told me the story of three men coming into his office and putting a gun to his head. They wanted to know where his cash was. My father always dealt with a lot of cash, and once a week it had to be deposited. Someone must have tipped them off. He said he didn't know what to do—he really needed to deposit that cash—for years he was just a deposit away from financial ruin. So he acted a faint. Is an acted faint a *feint*? He just dropped to the floor, as though he were out cold. Astonishingly, his act worked. The men left. I'm still a little stunned when I think of this story, partly in gratitude for my father's improvisatory skill, his thinking on his feet, and partly for the lack of persistence of those three stooges who gave up so easily. I mean, in the movies, by this time in the '60s, they would have picked him and roughed him up a little, right? They would have said something like, "Not so fast." But life isn't the movies. How often I need to remind myself of that. Sometimes, briefly, things end well.

Arbogast (the name is more memorable than the man: *Arbo-gasp*?) is literally a fall guy, part of the MacGuffin plot. He reminds us that bad things happen to neutral people, to everyone. Balsam was a character actor who played a lot of men whom we, colloquially, wouldn't think of as *characters*, men like my father who were colorful, elaborate, complicated in ways I never could fully understand.

Perhaps that, too, was why he called my father through

the years: a friend, yes, and a New York *character*, joke telling, street smart, philosophical, worldly, filled, as no doubt Balsam was, by Yiddishkeit. Who knows, perhaps one of his hardest roles was trying to *not* act like a Jewish guy from the Grand Concourse when he was in Beverly Hills. Perhaps on the phone to New York he didn't have to.

Martin Balsam died while on vacation in Rome in 1995. My father had retired by then, so he didn't book the ticket. He lived until 2017, and once in awhile he would say, "Poor Marty, at least he died in Rome." Whatever that means.

31192022042111

CPSIA information can be obtained
at www.ICGtesting.com
Printed in the USA
LVHW092035150820
663286LV00003B/123